# MAN'S SEARCH
# FOR MEANING

*Viktor E. Frankl, c. 1949*

IMAGNO/Viktor Frankl Institut

# MAN'S SEARCH FOR MEANING

## VIKTOR E. FRANKL

PART ONE TRANSLATED
BY ILSE LASCH

FOREWORD BY
HAROLD S. KUSHNER

AFTERWORD BY
WILLIAM J. WINSLADE

BEACON PRESS, BOSTON

BEACON PRESS
25 Beacon Street
Boston, Massachusetts 02108-2892
www. beacon.org

Beacon Press books are published under the auspices of
the Unitarian Universalist Association of Congregations.

© 1959, 1962, 1984, 1992, 2006 by Viktor E. Frankl
Foreword © 2006 by Harold S. Kushner
Afterword © 2006 by William J. Winslade
All rights reserved
Printed in the United States of America
First published in German in 1946 under the title
*Ein Psycholog erlebt das Konzentrationslager.*
Original English title was *From Death-Camp to Existentialism.*

09 08 07 06   8 7 6 5 4 3 2

Text design by Tag Savage
Composition by Wilsted & Taylor Publishing Services

LIBRARY OF CONGRESS CATALOGING-IN-PUBLICATION DATA

Frankl, Viktor Emil.
[Ein Psycholog erlebt das Konzentrationslager. English]
Man's search for meaning: an introduction to logotherapy /
Viktor E. Frankl; part one translated by Ilse Lasch
   p.   cm.
ISBN 0-8070-1426-5 (cloth : alk. paper)
1. Frankl, Viktor Emil. 2. Holocaust, Jewish (1939–1945)—
Personal narratives. 3. Holocaust, Jewish (1939–1945)—
Psychological aspects. 4. Psychologists—Austria—Biography.
5. Logotherapy. I. Title.
D810.J4F72713 1992
150.19'5—DC20 92-21055

*To the
memory of
my mother*

# CONTENTS

# FOREWORD

VIKTOR FRANKL'S *Man's Search for Meaning* is one of the great books of our time. Typically, if a book has one passage, one idea with the power to change a person's life, that alone justifies reading it, rereading it, and finding room for it on one's shelves. This book has several such passages.

It is first of all a book about survival. Like so many German and East European Jews who thought themselves secure in the 1930s, Frankl was cast into the Nazi network of concentration and extermination camps. Miraculously, he survived, in the biblical phrase "a brand plucked from the fire." But his account in this book is less about his travails, what he suffered and lost, than it is about the sources of his strength to survive. Several times in the course of the book, Frankl approvingly quotes the words of Nietzsche: "He who has a Why to live for can bear almost any How." He describes poignantly those prisoners who gave up on life, who had lost all hope for a future and were inevitably the first to die. They died less from lack of food or medicine than from lack of hope, lack of something to live for. By contrast, Frankl kept himself alive and kept hope alive by summoning up thoughts of his wife and the prospect of seeing her again, and by dreaming at one point of lecturing after the war about the psychological lessons to be learned from the Auschwitz experience. Clearly, many prisoners who desperately wanted to live did die, some from disease, some in the crematoria. But Frankl's concern is less with the question of why most died than it is with the question of why anyone at all survived.

Terrible as it was, his experience in Auschwitz reinforced what was already one of his key ideas: Life is not primarily a quest for pleasure, as Freud believed, or a quest for power, as Alfred Adler taught, but a quest for meaning. The greatest task for any person is to find meaning in his or her life. Frankl saw three possible sources for meaning: in work (doing something significant), in love (caring for another person), and in courage during difficult times. Suffering in and of itself is meaningless; we give our suffering meaning by the way in which we respond to it. At one point, Frankl writes that a person "may remain brave, dignified and unselfish, or in the bitter fight for self-preservation he may forget his human dignity and become no more than an animal." He concedes that only a few prisoners of the Nazis were able to do the former, "but even one such example is sufficient proof that man's inner strength may raise him above his outward fate."

Finally, Frankl's most enduring insight, one that I have called on often in my own life and in countless counseling situations: Forces beyond your control can take away everything you possess except one thing, your freedom to choose how you will respond to the situation. You cannot control what happens to you in life, but you can always control what you will feel and do about what happens to you.

There is a scene in Arthur Miller's play *Incident at Vichy* in which an upper-middle-class professional man appears before the Nazi authority that has occupied his town and shows his credentials: his university degrees, his letters of reference from prominent citizens, and so on. The Nazi asks him, "Is that everything you have?" The man nods. The Nazi throws it all in the wastebasket and tells him: "Good, now you have nothing." The man, whose self-esteem had always depended on the respect of others, is emotionally destroyed. Frankl would have argued that we are never left with nothing as long as we retain the freedom to choose how we will respond.

My own congregational experience has shown me the truth of Frankl's insights. I have known successful businessmen who, upon retirement, lost all zest for life. Their work had given their lives meaning. Often it was the only thing that had given their lives meaning and, without it, they spent day after day sitting at home, depressed, "with nothing to do." I have known people who rose to the challenge of enduring the most terrible afflictions and situations as long as they believed there was a point to their suffering. Whether it was a family milestone they wanted to live long enough to share or the prospect of doctors finding a cure by studying their illness, having a Why to live for enabled them to bear the How.

And my own experience echoes Frankl's in another way. Just as the ideas in my book *When Bad Things Happen to Good People* gained power and credibility because they were offered in the context of my struggle to understand the illness and death of our son, Frankl's doctrine of logotherapy, curing the soul by leading it to find meaning in life, gains credibility against the background of his anguish in Auschwitz. The last half of the book without the first would be far less effective.

I find it significant that the Foreword to the 1962 edition of

*Man's Search for Meaning* was written by a prominent psychologist, Dr. Gordon Allport, and the Foreword to this new edition is written by a clergyman. We have come to recognize that this is a profoundly religious book. It insists that life is meaningful and that we must learn to see life as meaningful despite our circumstances. It emphasizes that there is an ultimate purpose to life. And in its original version, before a postscript was added, it concluded with one of the most religious sentences written in the twentieth century:

> We have come to know Man as he really is. After all, man is that being who invented the gas chambers of Auschwitz; however, he is also that being who entered those gas chambers upright, with the Lord's Prayer or the *Shema Yisrael* on his lips.

HAROLD S. KUSHNER

*Harold S. Kushner is rabbi emeritus at Temple Israel in Natick, Massachusetts, and the author of several best-selling books, including* When Bad Things Happen to Good People, Living a Life That Matters, *and* When All You've Ever Wanted Isn't Enough.

# PREFACE TO
# THE 1992 EDITION

THIS BOOK HAS NOW LIVED TO SEE nearly one hundred print-
ings in English—in addition to having been published in
twenty-one other languages. And the English editions alone
have sold more than three million copies.

These are the dry facts, and they may well be the reason
why reporters of American newspapers and particularly of
American TV stations more often than not start their interviews, after listing these facts, by exclaiming: "Dr. Frankl, your
book has become a true bestseller—how do you feel about
such a success?" Whereupon I react by reporting that in the
first place I do not at all see in the bestseller status of my book
an achievement and accomplishment on my part but rather
an expression of the misery of our time: if hundreds of thousands of people reach out for a book whose very title prom-
ises to deal with the question of a meaning to life, it must be
a question that burns under their fingernails.

To be sure, something else may have contributed to the
impact of the book: its second, theoretical part ("Logotherapy in a Nutshell") boils down, as it were, to the lesson one
may distill from the first part, the autobiographical account
("Experiences in a Concentration Camp"), whereas Part One

serves as the existential validation of my theories. Thus, both parts mutually support their credibility.

I had none of this in mind when I wrote the book in 1945. And I did so within nine successive days and with the firm determination that the book should be published anonymously. In fact, the first printing of the original German version does not show my name on the cover, though at the last moment, just before the book's initial publication, I did finally give in to my friends who had urged me to let it be published with my name at least on the title page. At first, however, it had been written with the absolute conviction that, as an anonymous opus, it could never earn its author literary fame. I had wanted simply to convey to the reader by way of a concrete example that life holds a potential meaning under any conditions, even the most miserable ones. And I thought that if the point were demonstrated in a situation as extreme as that in a concentration camp, my book might gain a hearing. I therefore felt responsible for writing down what I had gone through, for I thought it might be helpful to people who are prone to despair.

And so it is both strange and remarkable to me that—among some dozens of books I have authored—precisely this one, which I had intended to be published anonymously so that it could never build up any reputation on the part of the author, did become a success. Again and again I therefore admonish my students both in Europe and in America: "Don't aim at success—the more you aim at it and make it a target, the more you are going to miss it. For success, like happiness, cannot be pursued; it must ensue, and it only does so as the unintended side-effect of one's dedication to a cause greater than oneself or as the by-product of one's surrender to a person other than oneself. Happiness must happen, and the same holds for success: you have to let it happen by not caring about it. I want you to listen to what your conscience commands you to do and go on to carry it out to the best of your knowledge. Then you will live to see that in the long run—in the long run, I say!—success will follow you precisely because you had *forgotten* to think of it."

The reader may ask me why I did not try to escape what was in store for me after Hitler had occupied Austria. Let me answer by recalling the following story. Shortly before the United States entered World War II, I received an invitation to come to the American Consulate in Vienna to pick up my immigration visa. My old parents were overjoyed because they expected that I would soon be allowed to leave Austria. I suddenly hesitated, however. The question beset me: could I really afford to leave my parents alone to face their fate, to be sent, sooner or later, to a concentration camp, or even to a so-called extermination camp? Where did my responsibility lie? Should I foster my brain child, logotherapy, by emigrating to fertile soil where I could write my books? Or should I concentrate on my duties as a real child, the child of my parents who had to do whatever he could to protect them? I pondered the problem this way and that but could not arrive at a solution; this was the type of dilemma that made one wish for "a hint from Heaven," as the phrase goes.

It was then that I noticed a piece of marble lying on a table at home. When I asked my father about it, he explained that he had found it on the site where the National Socialists had burned down the largest Viennese synagogue. He had taken the piece home because it was a part of the tablets on which the Ten Commandments were inscribed. One gilded Hebrew letter was engraved on the piece; my father explained that this letter stood for one of the Commandments. Eagerly I asked, "Which one is it?" He answered, "Honor thy father and thy mother that thy days may be long upon the land." At that moment I decided to stay with my father and my mother upon the land, and to let the American visa lapse.

VIKTOR E. FRANKL
*Vienna, 1992*

# MAN'S SEARCH FOR MEANING

I

# EXPERIENCES IN A
# CONCENTRATION CAMP

THIS BOOK DOES NOT CLAIM TO BE an account of facts and events but of personal experiences, experiences which millions of prisoners have suffered time and again. It is the inside story of a concentration camp, told by one of its survivors. This tale is not concerned with the great horrors, which have already been described often enough (though less often believed), but with the multitude of small torments. In other words, it will try to answer this question: How was everyday life in a concentration camp reflected in the mind of the average prisoner?

Most of the events described here did not take place in the large and famous camps, but in the small ones where most of the real extermination took place. This story is not about the suffering and death of great heroes and martyrs, nor is it about the prominent Capos—prisoners who acted as trustees, having special privileges—or well-known prisoners. Thus it is not so much concerned with the sufferings of the mighty, but with the sacrifices, the crucifixion and the deaths of the great army of unknown and unrecorded victims. It was these common prisoners, who bore no distinguishing marks on their sleeves, whom the Capos really despised. While these ordinary prisoners had little or nothing to eat, the Capos were never hungry; in fact many of the Capos fared better in the camp than they had in their entire lives. Often they were harder on the prisoners than were the guards, and beat them more cruelly than the SS men did. These Capos, of course, were chosen only from those prisoners whose characters promised to make them suitable for such procedures, and if they did not comply with what was expected of them, they were immediately demoted. They soon became much like the SS men and the camp wardens and may be judged on a similar psychological basis.

It is easy for the outsider to get the wrong conception of camp life, a conception mingled with sentiment and pity. Little does he know of the hard fight for existence which raged among the prisoners. This was an unrelenting struggle for daily bread and for life itself, for one's own sake or for that of a good friend.

Let us take the case of a transport which was officially announced to transfer a certain number of prisoners to another camp; but it was a fairly safe guess that its final destination would be the gas chambers. A selection of sick or feeble prisoners incapable of work would be sent to one of the big central camps which were fitted with gas chambers and crematoriums. The selection process was the signal for a free fight among all the prisoners, or of group against group. All that mattered was that one's own name and that of one's friend were crossed off the list of victims, though everyone knew that for each man saved another victim had to be found.

A definite number of prisoners had to go with each transport. It did not really matter which, since each of them was nothing but a number. On their admission to the camp (at least this was the method in Auschwitz) all their documents had been taken from them, together with their other possessions. Each prisoner, therefore, had had an opportunity to claim a fictitious name or profession; and for various reasons many did this. The authorities were interested only in the captives' numbers. These numbers were often tattooed on their skin, and also had to be sewn to a certain spot on the trousers, jacket, or coat. Any guard who wanted to make a charge against a prisoner just glanced at his number (and how we dreaded such glances!); he never asked for his name.

To return to the convoy about to depart. There was neither time nor desire to consider moral or ethical issues. Every man was controlled by one thought only: to keep himself alive for the family waiting for him at home, and to save his friends. With no hesitation, therefore, he would arrange for another prisoner, another "number," to take his place in the transport.

As I have already mentioned, the process of selecting Capos was a negative one; only the most brutal of the prisoners were chosen for this job (although there were some happy exceptions). But apart from the selection of Capos which was undertaken by the SS, there was a sort of self-selecting process going on the whole time among all of the prisoners. On the average, only those prisoners could keep alive who, after years of trekking from camp to camp, had lost all scruples in their fight for existence; they were prepared to use every means, honest and otherwise, even brutal force, theft, and betrayal of their friends, in order to save themselves. We who have come back, by the aid of many lucky chances or miracles—whatever one may choose to call them—we know: the best of us did not return.

Many factual accounts about concentration camps are already on record. Here, facts will be significant only as far as they are part of a man's experiences. It is the exact nature of these experiences that the following essay will attempt to describe. For those who have been inmates in a camp, it will attempt to explain their experiences in the light of present-day knowledge. And for those who have never been inside, it may help them to comprehend, and above all to understand, the experiences of that only too small percentage of prisoners who survived and who now find life very difficult. These former prisoners often say, "We dislike talking about our experiences. No explanations are needed for those who have been inside, and the others will understand neither how we felt then nor how we feel now."

To attempt a methodical presentation of the subject is very difficult, as psychology requires a certain scientific detachment. But does a man who makes his observations while he himself is a prisoner possess the necessary detachment? Such detachment is granted to the outsider, but he is too far removed to make any statements of real value. Only the man inside knows. His judgments may not be objective; his evaluations may be out of proportion. This is inevitable. An attempt must be made to avoid any personal bias, and that is the real difficulty of a book of this kind. At times it will be necessary to have the courage to tell of very intimate experiences. I had intended to write this book anonymously, using my prison number only. But when the manuscript was completed, I saw that as an anonymous publication it would lose half its value, and that I must have the courage to state my convictions openly. I therefore refrained from deleting any of the passages, in spite of an intense dislike of exhibitionism.

I shall leave it to others to distill the contents of this book into dry theories. These might become a contribution to the psychology of prison life, which was investigated after the First World War, and which acquainted us with the syndrome of "barbed wire sickness." We are indebted to the Second World War for enriching our knowledge of the "psychopathology of the masses" (if I may quote a variation of the well-known phrase and title of a book by LeBon), for the war gave us the war of nerves and it gave us the concentration camp.

As this story is about my experiences as an ordinary prisoner, it is important that I mention, not without pride, that I was not employed as a psychiatrist in camp, or even as a doctor, except for the last few weeks. A few of my colleagues were lucky enough to be employed in poorly heated first-aid posts applying bandages made of scraps of waste paper. But I was Number 119,104, and most of the time I was digging and laying tracks for railway lines. At one time, my job was to dig a tunnel, without help, for a water main under a road. This feat did not go unrewarded; just before Christmas 1944, I was presented with a gift of so-called "premium coupons." These were issued by the construction firm to which we were practically sold as slaves: the firm paid the camp authorities a fixed price per day, per prisoner. The coupons cost the firm fifty pfennigs each and could be exchanged for six cigarettes, often weeks later, although they sometimes lost their validity. I became the proud owner of a token worth twelve cigarettes. But more important, the cigarettes could be exchanged for twelve soups, and twelve soups were often a very real respite from starvation.

The privilege of actually smoking cigarettes was reserved for the Capo, who had his assured quota of weekly coupons; or possibly for a prisoner who worked as a foreman in a warehouse or workshop and received a few cigarettes in exchange for doing dangerous jobs. The only exceptions to this were those who had lost the will to live and wanted to "enjoy" their last days. Thus, when we saw a comrade smoking his own cigarettes, we knew he had given up faith in his strength to carry on, and, once lost, the will to live seldom returned.

When one examines the vast amount of material which has been amassed as the result of many prisoners' observations and experiences, three phases of the inmate's mental reactions to camp life become apparent: the period following his admission; the period when he is well entrenched in camp routine; and the period following his release and liberation.

The symptom that characterizes the first phase is shock. Under certain conditions shock may even precede the prisoner's formal admission to the camp. I shall give as an example the circumstances of my own admission.

Fifteen hundred persons had been traveling by train for several days and nights: there were eighty people in each coach. All had to lie on top of their luggage, the few remnants of their personal possessions. The carriages were so full that only the top parts of the windows were free to let in the grey of dawn. Everyone expected the train to head for some munitions factory, in which we would be employed as forced labor. We did not know whether we were still in Silesia or already in Poland. The engine's whistle had an uncanny sound, like a cry for help sent out in commiseration for the unhappy load which it was destined to lead into perdition. Then the train shunted, obviously nearing a main station. Suddenly a cry broke from the ranks of the anxious passengers, "There is a sign, Auschwitz!" Everyone's heart missed a beat at that moment. Auschwitz—the very name stood for all that was horrible: gas chambers, crematoriums, massacres. Slowly, almost hesitatingly, the train moved on as if it wanted to spare its passengers the dreadful realization as long as possible: Auschwitz!

With the progressive dawn, the outlines of an immense camp became visible: long stretches of several rows of barbed wire fences; watch towers; searchlights; and long columns of ragged human figures, grey in the greyness of dawn, trekking along the straight desolate roads, to what destination we did not know. There were isolated shouts and whistles of command. We did not know their meaning. My imagination led me to see gallows with people dangling on them. I was horrified, but this was just as well, because step by step we had to become accustomed to a terrible and immense horror.

Eventually we moved into the station. The initial silence was interrupted by shouted commands. We were to hear those rough, shrill tones from then on, over and over again in all the camps. Their sound was almost like the last cry of a victim, and yet there was a difference. It had a rasping hoarseness, as if it came from the throat of a man who had to keep shouting like that, a man who was being murdered again and again. The carriage doors were flung open and a small detachment of prisoners stormed inside. They wore striped uniforms, their heads were shaved, but they looked well fed. They spoke in every possible European tongue, and all with a certain amount of humor, which sounded grotesque under the circumstances. Like a drowning man clutching a straw, my inborn optimism (which has often controlled my feelings even in the most desperate situations) clung to this thought: These prisoners look quite well, they seem to be in good spirits and even laugh. Who knows? I might manage to share their favorable position.

In psychiatry there is a certain condition known as "delusion of reprieve." The condemned man, immediately before his execution, gets the illusion that he might be reprieved at the very last minute. We, too, clung to shreds of hope and believed to the last moment that it would not be so bad. Just the sight of the red cheeks and round faces of those prisoners was a great encouragement. Little did we know then that they formed a specially chosen elite, who for years had been the receiving squad for new transports as they rolled into the station day after day. They took charge of the new arrivals and their luggage, including scarce items and smuggled jewelry. Auschwitz must have been a strange spot in this Europe of the last years of the war. There must have been unique treasures of gold and silver, platinum and diamonds, not only in the huge storehouses but also in the hands of the SS.

Fifteen hundred captives were cooped up in a shed built to accommodate probably two hundred at the most. We were cold and hungry and there was not enough room for everyone to squat on the bare ground, let alone to lie down. One five-ounce piece of bread was our only food in four days. Yet I heard the senior prisoners in charge of the shed bargain with one member of the receiving party about a tie-pin made of platinum and diamonds. Most of the profits would eventually be traded for liquor—schnapps. I do not remember any more just how many thousands of marks were needed to purchase the quantity of schnapps required for a "gay evening," but I do know that those long-term prisoners needed schnapps. Under such conditions, who could blame them for trying to dope themselves? There was another group of prisoners who got liquor supplied in almost unlimited quantities by the SS: these were the men who were employed in the gas chambers and crematoriums, and who knew very well that one day they would be relieved by a new shift of men, and that they would have to leave their enforced role of executioner and become victims themselves.

Nearly everyone in our transport lived under the illusion that he would be reprieved, that everything would yet be well. We did not realize the meaning behind the scene that was to follow presently. We were told to leave our luggage in the train and to fall into two lines—women on one side, men on the other—in order to file past a senior SS officer. Surprisingly enough, I had the courage to hide my haversack under my coat. My line filed past the officer, man by man. I realized that it would be dangerous if the officer spotted my bag. He would at least knock me down; I knew that from previous experience. Instinctively, I straightened on approaching the officer, so that he would not notice my heavy load. Then I was face to face with him. He was a tall man who looked slim and fit in his spotless uniform. What a contrast to us, who were untidy and grimy after our long journey! He had assumed an attitude of careless ease, supporting his right elbow with his left hand. His right hand was lifted, and with the forefinger of that hand he pointed very leisurely to the right or to the left. None of us had the slightest idea of the sinister meaning behind that little movement of a man's finger, pointing now to the right and now to the left, but far more frequently to the left.

It was my turn. Somebody whispered to me that to be sent to the right side would mean work, the way to the left being for the sick and those incapable of work, who would be sent to a special camp. I just waited for things to take their course, the first of many such times to come. My haversack weighed me down a bit to the left, but I made an effort to walk upright. The SS man looked me over, appeared to hesitate, then put both his hands on my shoulders. I tried very hard to look smart, and he turned my shoulders very slowly until I faced right, and I moved over to that side.

The significance of the finger game was explained to us in the evening. It was the first selection, the first verdict made on our existence or non-existence. For the great majority of our transport, about 90 percent, it meant death. Their sentence was carried out within the next few hours. Those who were sent to the left were marched from the station straight to the crematorium. This building, as I was told by someone who worked there, had the word "bath" written over its doors in several European languages. On entering, each prisoner was handed a piece of soap, and then—but mercifully I do not need to describe the events which followed. Many accounts have been written about this horror.

We who were saved, the minority of our transport, found out the truth in the evening. I inquired from prisoners who had been there for some time where my colleague and friend P—— had been sent.

"Was he sent to the left side?"

"Yes," I replied.

"Then you can see him there," I was told.

"Where?" A hand pointed to the chimney a few hundred yards off, which was sending a column of flame up into the grey sky of Poland. It dissolved into a sinister cloud of smoke.

"That's where your friend is, floating up to Heaven," was the answer. But I still did not understand until the truth was explained to me in plain words.

But I am telling things out of their turn. From a psychological point of view, we had a long, long way in front of us from the break of that dawn at the station until our first night's rest at the camp.

Escorted by SS guards with loaded guns, we were made to run from the station, past electrically charged barbed wire, through the camp, to the cleansing station; for those of us who had passed the first selection, this was a real bath. Again our illusion of reprieve found confirmation. The SS men seemed almost charming. Soon we found out their reason. They were nice to us as long as they saw watches on our wrists and could persuade us in well-meaning tones to hand them over. Would we not have to hand over all our possessions anyway, and why should not that relatively nice person have the watch? Maybe one day he would do one a good turn.

We waited in a shed which seemed to be the anteroom to the disinfecting chamber. SS men appeared and spread out blankets into which we had to throw all our possessions, all our watches and jewelry. There were still naïve prisoners among us who asked, to the amusement of the more seasoned ones who were there as helpers, if they could not keep a wedding ring, a medal or a good-luck piece. No one could yet grasp the fact that everything would be taken away.

I tried to take one of the old prisoners into my confidence. Approaching him furtively, I pointed to the roll of paper in the inner pocket of my coat and said, "Look, this is the manuscript of a scientific book. I know what you will say; that I should be grateful to escape with my life, that that should be all I can expect of fate. But I cannot help myself. I must keep this manuscript at all costs; it contains my life's work. Do you understand that?"

Yes, he was beginning to understand. A grin spread slowly over his face, first piteous, then more amused, mocking, insulting, until he bellowed one word at me in answer to my question, a word that was ever present in the vocabulary of the camp inmates: "Shit!" At that moment I saw the plain truth and did what marked the culminating point of the first phase of my psychological reaction: I struck out my whole former life.

Suddenly there was a stir among my fellow travelers, who had been standing about with pale, frightened faces, helplessly debating. Again we heard the hoarsely shouted commands. We were driven with blows into the immediate anteroom of the bath. There we assembled around an SS man who waited until we had all arrived. Then he said, "I will give you two minutes, and I shall time you by my watch. In these two minutes you will get fully undressed and drop everything on the floor where you are standing. You will take nothing with you except your shoes, your belt or suspenders, and possibly a truss. I am starting to count—now!"

With unthinkable haste, people tore off their clothes. As the time grew shorter, they became increasingly nervous and pulled clumsily at their underwear, belts and shoelaces. Then we heard the first sounds of whipping; leather straps beating down on naked bodies.

Next we were herded into another room to be shaved: not only our heads were shorn, but not a hair was left on our entire bodies. Then on to the showers, where we lined up again. We hardly recognized each other; but with great relief some people noted that real water dripped from the sprays.

While we were waiting for the shower, our nakedness was brought home to us: we really had nothing now except our bare bodies—even minus hair; all we possessed, literally, was our naked existence. What else remained for us as a material link with our former lives? For me there were my glasses and my belt; the latter I had to exchange later on for a piece of bread. There was an extra bit of excitement in store for the owners of trusses. In the evening the senior prisoner in charge of our hut welcomed us with a speech in which he gave us his word of honor that he would hang, personally, "from that beam"—he pointed to it—any person who had sewn money or precious stones into his truss. Proudly he explained that as a senior inhabitant the camp laws entitled him to do so.

Where our shoes were concerned, matters were not so simple. Although we were supposed to keep them, those who had fairly decent pairs had to give them up after all and were given in exchange shoes that did not fit. In for real trouble were those prisoners who had followed the apparently well-meant advice (given in the anteroom) of the senior prisoners and had shortened their jackboots by cutting the tops off, then smearing soap on the cut edges to hide the sabotage. The SS men seemed to have waited for just that. All suspected of this crime had to go into a small adjoining room. After a time we again heard the lashings of the strap, and the screams of tortured men. This time it lasted for quite a while.

Thus the illusions some of us still held were destroyed one by one, and then, quite unexpectedly, most of us were overcome by a grim sense of humor. We knew that we had nothing to lose except our so ridiculously naked lives. When the showers started to run, we all tried very hard to make fun, both about ourselves and about each other. After all, real water did flow from the sprays!

Apart from that strange kind of humor, another sensation seized us: curiosity. I have experienced this kind of curiosity before, as a fundamental reaction toward certain strange circumstances. When my life was once endangered by a climbing accident, I felt only one sensation at the critical moment: curiosity, curiosity as to whether I should come out of it alive or with a fractured skull or some other injuries.

Cold curiosity predominated even in Auschwitz, somehow detaching the mind from its surroundings, which came to be regarded with a kind of objectivity. At that time one cultivated this state of mind as a means of protection. We were anxious to know what would happen next; and what would be the consequence, for example, of our standing in the open air, in the chill of late autumn, stark naked, and still wet from the showers. In the next few days our curiosity evolved into surprise; surprise that we did not catch cold.

There were many similar surprises in store for new arrivals. The medical men among us learned first of all: "Textbooks tell lies!" Somewhere it is said that man cannot exist without sleep for more than a stated number of hours. Quite wrong! I had been convinced that there were certain things I just could not do: I could not sleep without this or I could not live with that or the other. The first night in Auschwitz we slept in beds which were constructed in tiers. On each tier (measuring about six-and-a-half to eight feet) slept nine men, directly on the boards. Two blankets were shared by each nine men. We could, of course, lie only on our sides, crowded and huddled against each other, which had some advantages because of the bitter cold. Though it was forbidden to take shoes up to the bunks, some people did use them secretly as pillows in spite of the fact that they were caked with mud. Otherwise one's head had to rest on the crook of an almost dislocated arm. And yet sleep came and brought oblivion and relief from pain for a few hours.

I would like to mention a few similar surprises on how much we could endure: we were unable to clean our teeth, and yet, in spite of that and a severe vitamin deficiency, we had healthier gums than ever before. We had to wear the same shirts for half a year, until they had lost all appearance of being shirts. For days we were unable to wash, even partially, because of frozen water-pipes, and yet the sores and abrasions on hands which were dirty from work in the soil did not suppurate (that is, unless there was frostbite). Or for instance, a light sleeper, who used to be disturbed by the slightest noise in the next room, now found himself lying pressed against a comrade who snored loudly a few inches from his ear and yet slept quite soundly through the noise.

If someone now asked of us the truth of Dostoevski's statement that flatly defines man as a being who can get used to anything, we would reply, "Yes, a man can get used to anything, but do not ask us how." But our psychological investigations have not taken us that far yet; neither had we prisoners reached that point. We were still in the first phase of our psychological reactions.

The thought of suicide was entertained by nearly everyone, if only for a brief time. It was born of the hopelessness of the situation, the constant danger of death looming over us daily and hourly, and the closeness of the deaths suffered by many of the others. From personal convictions which will be mentioned later, I made myself a firm promise, on my first evening in camp, that I would not "run into the wire." This was a phrase used in camp to describe the most popular method of suicide—touching the electrically charged barbed-wire fence. It was not entirely difficult for me to make this decision. There was little point in committing suicide, since, for the average inmate, life expectation, calculating objectively and counting all likely chances, was very poor. He could not with any assurance expect to be among the small percentage of men who survived all the selections. The prisoner of Auschwitz, in the first phase of shock, did not fear death. Even the gas chambers lost their horrors for him after the first few days—after all, they spared him the act of committing suicide.

Friends whom I have met later have told me that I was not

one of those whom the shock of admission greatly depressed. I only smiled, and quite sincerely, when the following episode occurred the morning after our first night in Auschwitz. In spite of strict orders not to leave our "blocks," a colleague of mine, who had arrived in Auschwitz several weeks previously, smuggled himself into our hut. He wanted to calm and comfort us and tell us a few things. He had become so thin that at first we did not recognize him. With a show of good humor and a devil-may-care attitude he gave us a few hurried tips: "Don't be afraid! Don't fear the selections! Dr. M—— (the SS medical chief) has a soft spot for doctors." (This was wrong; my friend's kindly words were misleading. One prisoner, the doctor of a block of huts and a man of some sixty years, told me how he had entreated Dr. M—— to let off his son, who was destined for gas. Dr. M—— coldly refused.)

"But one thing I beg of you"; he continued, "shave daily, if at all possible, even if you have to use a piece of glass to do it ... even if you have to give your last piece of bread for it. You will look younger and the scraping will make your cheeks look ruddier. If you want to stay alive, there is only one way: look fit for work. If you even limp, because, let us say, you have a small blister on your heel, and an SS man spots this, he will wave you aside and the next day you are sure to be gassed. Do you know what we mean by a 'Moslem'? A man who looks miserable, down and out, sick and emaciated, and who cannot manage hard physical labor any longer ... that is a 'Moslem.' Sooner or later, usually sooner, every 'Moslem' goes to the gas chambers. Therefore, remember: shave, stand and walk smartly; then you need not be afraid of gas. All of you standing here, even if you have only been here twenty-four hours, you need not fear gas, except perhaps you." And then he pointed to me and said, "I hope you don't mind my telling you frankly." To the others he repeated, "Of all of you he is the only one who must fear the next selection. So, don't worry!"

And I smiled. I am now convinced that anyone in my place on that day would have done the same.

I think it was Lessing who once said, "There are things which must cause you to lose your reason or you have none to lose." An abnormal reaction to an abnormal situation is normal behavior. Even we psychiatrists expect the reactions of a man to an abnormal situation, such as being committed to an asylum, to be abnormal in proportion to the degree of his normality. The reaction of a man to his admission to a concentration camp also represents an abnormal state of mind, but judged objectively it is a normal and, as will be shown later, typical reaction to the given circumstances. These reactions, as I have described them, began to change in a few days. The prisoner passed from the first to the second phase; the phase of relative apathy, in which he achieved a kind of emotional death.

Apart from the already described reactions, the newly arrived prisoner experienced the tortures of other most painful emotions, all of which he tried to deaden. First of all, there was his boundless longing for his home and his family. This often could become so acute that he felt himself consumed by longing. Then there was disgust; disgust with all the ugliness which surrounded him, even in its mere external forms.

Most of the prisoners were given a uniform of rags which would have made a scarecrow elegant by comparison. Be-

MAN'S SEARCH FOR MEANING

tween the huts in the camp lay pure filth, and the more one worked to clear it away, the more one had to come in contact with it. It was a favorite practice to detail a new arrival to a work group whose job was to clean the latrines and remove the sewage. If, as usually happened, some of the excrement splashed into his face during its transport over bumpy fields, any sign of disgust by the prisoner or any attempt to wipe off the filth would only be punished with a blow from a Capo. And thus the mortification of normal reactions was hastened.

At first the prisoner looked away if he saw the punishment parades of another group; he could not bear to see fellow prisoners march up and down for hours in the mire, their movements directed by blows. Days or weeks later things changed. Early in the morning, when it was still dark, the prisoner stood in front of the gate with his detachment, ready to march. He heard a scream and saw how a comrade was knocked down, pulled to his feet again, and knocked down once more—and why? He was feverish but had reported to sick-bay at an improper time. He was being punished for this irregular attempt to be relieved of his duties.

But the prisoner who had passed into the second stage of his psychological reactions did not avert his eyes any more. By then his feelings were blunted, and he watched unmoved. Another example: he found himself waiting at sick-bay, hoping to be granted two days of light work inside the camp because of injuries or perhaps edema or fever. He stood unmoved while a twelve-year-old boy was carried in who had been forced to stand at attention for hours in the snow or to work outside with bare feet because there were no shoes for him in the camp. His toes had become frostbitten, and the doctor on duty picked off the black gangrenous stumps with tweezers, one by one. Disgust, horror and pity are emotions that our spectator could not really feel any more. The sufferers, the dying and the dead, became such commonplace sights to him after a few weeks of camp life that they could not move him any more.

I spent some time in a hut for typhus patients who ran very high temperatures and were often delirious, many of them moribund. After one of them had just died, I watched without any emotional upset the scene that followed, which was repeated over and over again with each death. One by one the prisoners approached the still warm body. One grabbed the remains of a messy meal of potatoes; another decided that the corpse's wooden shoes were an improvement on his own, and exchanged them. A third man did the same with the dead man's coat, and another was glad to be able to secure some—just imagine!—genuine string.

All this I watched with unconcern. Eventually I asked the "nurse" to remove the body. When he decided to do so, he took the corpse by its legs, allowing it to drop into the small corridor between the two rows of boards which were the beds for the fifty typhus patients, and dragged it across the bumpy earthen floor toward the door. The two steps which led up into the open air always constituted a problem for us, since we were exhausted from a chronic lack of food. After a few months' stay in the camp we could not walk up those steps, which were each about six inches high, without putting our hands on the door jambs to pull ourselves up.

The man with the corpse approached the steps. Wearily he dragged himself up. Then the body: first the feet, then the trunk, and finally—with an uncanny rattling noise—the head of the corpse bumped up the two steps.

My place was on the opposite side of the hut, next to the small, sole window, which was built near the floor. While my cold hands clasped a bowl of hot soup from which I sipped greedily, I happened to look out the window. The corpse which had just been removed stared in at me with glazed eyes. Two hours before I had spoken to that man. Now I continued sipping my soup.

If my lack of emotion had not surprised me from the standpoint of professional interest, I would not remember this incident now, because there was so little feeling involved in it.

Apathy, the blunting of the emotions and the feeling that one could not care any more, were the symptoms arising during the second stage of the prisoner's psychological reactions, and which eventually made him insensitive to daily and hourly beatings. By means of this insensibility the prisoner soon surrounded himself with a very necessary protective shell.

Beatings occurred on the slightest provocation, sometimes for no reason at all. For example, bread was rationed out at our work site and we had to line up for it. Once, the man behind me stood off a little to one side and that lack of symmetry displeased the SS guard. I did not know what was going on in the line behind me, nor in the mind of the SS guard, but suddenly I received two sharp blows on my head. Only then did I spot the guard at my side who was using his stick. At such a moment it is not the physical pain which hurts the most (and this applies to adults as much as to punished children); it is the mental agony caused by the injustice, the un-reasonableness of it all.

Strangely enough, a blow which does not even find its mark can, under certain circumstances, hurt more than one that finds its mark. Once I was standing on a railway track in a snowstorm. In spite of the weather our party had to keep on working. I worked quite hard at mending the track with gravel, since that was the only way to keep warm. For only one moment I paused to get my breath and to lean on my shovel. Unfortunately the guard turned around just then and thought I was loafing. The pain he caused me was not from any insults or any blows. That guard did not think it worth his while to say anything, not even a swear word, to the ragged, emaciated figure standing before him, which probably re-minded him only vaguely of a human form. Instead, he play-fully picked up a stone and threw it at me. That, to me, seemed the way to attract the attention of a beast, to call a domestic animal back to its job, a creature with which you have so lit-tle in common that you do not even punish it.

The most painful part of beatings is the insult which they imply. At one time we had to carry some long, heavy girders over icy tracks. If one man slipped, he endangered not only himself but all the others who carried the same girder. An old friend of mine had a congenitally dislocated hip. He was glad to be capable of working in spite of it, since the physically dis-abled were almost certainly sent to death when a selection took place. He limped over the track with an especially heavy girder, and seemed about to fall and drag the others with him. As yet, I was not carrying a girder so I jumped to his as-sistance without stopping to think. I was immediately hit on the back, rudely reprimanded and ordered to return to my place. A few minutes previously the same guard who struck me had told us deprecatingly that we "pigs" lacked the spirit of comradeship.

Another time, in a forest, with the temperature at 2°F, we began to dig up the topsoil, which was frozen hard, in order to lay water pipes. By then I had grown rather weak physically. Along came a foreman with chubby rosy cheeks. His face definitely reminded me of a pig's head. I noticed that he wore lovely warm gloves in that bitter cold. For a time he watched me silently. I felt that trouble was brewing, for in front of me lay the mound of earth which showed exactly how much I had dug.

Then he began: "You pig, I have been watching you the whole time! I'll teach you to work, yet! Wait till you dig dirt with your teeth—you'll die like an animal! In two days I'll finish you off! You've never done a stroke of work in your life. What were you, swine? A businessman?"

I was past caring. But I had to take his threat of killing me seriously, so I straightened up and looked him directly in the eye. "I was a doctor—a specialist."

"What? A doctor? I bet you got a lot of money out of people."

"As it happens, I did most of my work for no money at all, in clinics for the poor." But, now, I had said too much. He threw himself on me and knocked me down, shouting like a madman. I can no longer remember what he shouted.

I want to show with this apparently trivial story that there are moments when indignation can rouse even a seemingly hardened prisoner—indignation not about cruelty or pain, but about the insult connected with it. That time blood rushed to my head because I had to listen to a man judge my life who had so little idea of it, a man (I must confess: the following remark, which I made to my fellow-prisoners after the scene, afforded me childish relief) "who looked so vulgar and brutal that the nurse in the out-patient ward in my hospital would not even have admitted him to the waiting room."

Fortunately the Capo in my working party was obligated to me; he had taken a liking to me because I listened to his love stories and matrimonial troubles, which he poured out during the long marches to our work site. I had made an impression on him with my diagnosis of his character and with my psychotherapeutic advice. After that he was grateful, and this had already been of value to me. On several previous occasions he had reserved a place for me next to him in one of the first five rows of our detachment, which usually consisted of two hundred and eighty men. That favor was important. We had to line up early in the morning while it was still dark. Everybody was afraid of being late and of having to stand in the back rows. If men were required for an unpleasant and disliked job, the senior Capo appeared and usually collected the men he needed from the back rows. These men had to march away to another, especially dreaded kind of work under the command of strange guards. Occasionally the senior Capo chose men from the first five rows, just to catch those who tried to be clever. All protests and entreaties were silenced by a few well-aimed kicks, and the chosen victims were chased to the meeting place with shouts and blows.

However, as long as my Capo felt the need of pouring out his heart, this could not happen to me. I had a guaranteed place of honor next to him. But there was another advantage, too. Like nearly all the camp inmates I was suffering from edema. My legs were so swollen and the skin on them so tightly stretched that I could scarcely bend my knees. I had to leave my shoes unlaced in order to make them fit my swollen feet. There would not have been space for socks even if I had had any. So my partly bare feet were always wet and my shoes always full of snow. This, of course, caused frostbite and chilblains. Every single step became real torture. Clumps of ice formed on our shoes during our marches over snow-covered fields. Over and again men slipped and those following behind stumbled on top of them. Then the column would stop for a moment, but not for long. One of the guards soon took action and worked over the men with the butt of his rifle to make them get up quickly. The more to the front of the column you were, the less often you were disturbed by having to stop and then to make up for lost time by running on your painful feet. I was very happy to be the personally appointed physician to His Honor the Capo, and to march in the first row at an even pace.

As an additional payment for my services, I could be sure that as long as soup was being dealt out at lunchtime at our work site, he would, when my turn came, dip the ladle right to the bottom of the vat and fish out a few peas. This Capo, a former army officer, even had the courage to whisper to the foreman, whom I had quarreled with, that he knew me to be an unusually good worker. That didn't help matters, but he nevertheless managed to save my life (one of the many times it was to be saved). The day after the episode with the foreman he smuggled me into another work party.

There were foremen who felt sorry for us and who did their best to ease our situation, at least at the building site. But even they kept on reminding us that an ordinary laborer did several times as much work as we did, and in a shorter time. But they did see reason if they were told that a normal workman did not live on 10½ ounces of bread (theoretically—actually we often had less) and 1¾ pints of thin soup per day; that a normal laborer did not live under the mental stress we had to submit to, not having news of our families, who had either been sent to another camp or gassed right away; that a normal workman was not threatened by death continuously, daily and hourly. I even allowed myself to say once to a kindly foreman, "If you could learn from me how to do a brain operation in as short a time as I am learning this road work from you, I would have great respect for you." And he grinned.

Apathy, the main symptom of the second phase, was a necessary mechanism of self-defense. Reality dimmed, and all efforts and all emotions were centered on one task: preserving one's own life and that of the other fellow. It was typical to hear the prisoners, while they were being herded back to camp from their work sites in the evening, sigh with relief and say, "Well, another day is over."

It can be readily understood that such a state of strain, coupled with the constant necessity of concentrating on the task of staying alive, forced the prisoner's inner life down to a primitive level. Several of my colleagues in camp who were trained in psychoanalysis often spoke of a "regression" in the camp inmate—a retreat to a more primitive form of mental life. His wishes and desires became obvious in his dreams.

What did the prisoner dream about most frequently? Of bread, cake, cigarettes, and nice warm baths. The lack of having these simple desires satisfied led him to seek wish-fulfillment in dreams. Whether these dreams did any good is another matter; the dreamer had to wake from them to the reality of camp life, and to the terrible contrast between that and his dream illusions.

I shall never forget how I was roused one night by the groans of a fellow prisoner, who threw himself about in his sleep, obviously having a horrible nightmare. Since I had always been especially sorry for people who suffered from fearful dreams or deliria, I wanted to wake the poor man. Suddenly I drew back the hand which was ready to shake him, frightened at the thing I was about to do. At that moment I became intensely conscious of the fact that no dream, no matter how horrible, could be as bad as the reality of the camp which surrounded us, and to which I was about to recall him.

Because of the high degree of undernourishment which the prisoners suffered, it was natural that the desire for food was the major primitive instinct around which mental life centered. Let us observe the majority of prisoners when they happened to work near each other and were, for once, not closely watched. They would immediately start discussing food. One fellow would ask another working next to him in the ditch what his favorite dishes were. Then they would exchange recipes and plan the menu for the day when they would have a reunion—the day in a distant future when they would be liberated and returned home. They would go on and on, picturing it all in detail, until suddenly a warning was passed down the trench, usually in the form of a special password or number: "The guard is coming."

I always regarded the discussions about food as dangerous. Is it not wrong to provoke the organism with such detailed and affective pictures of delicacies when it has somehow managed to adapt itself to extremely small rations and low calories? Though it may afford momentary psychological relief, it is an illusion which physiologically, surely, must not be without danger.

During the latter part of our imprisonment, the daily ration consisted of very watery soup given out once daily, and the usual small bread ration. In addition to that, there was the so-called "extra allowance," consisting of three-fourths of an ounce of margarine, or of a slice of poor quality sausage, or of a little piece of cheese, or a bit of synthetic honey, or a spoonful of watery jam, varying daily. In calories, this diet was absolutely inadequate, especially taking into consideration our heavy manual work and our constant exposure to the cold in inadequate clothing. The sick who were "under special care" —that is, those who were allowed to lie in the huts instead of leaving the camp for work—were even worse off.

When the last layers of subcutaneous fat had vanished, and we looked like skeletons disguised with skin and rags, we could watch our bodies beginning to devour themselves. The organism digested its own protein, and the muscles disappeared. Then the body had no powers of resistance left. One after another the members of the little community in our hut died. Each of us could calculate with fair accuracy whose turn would be next, and when his own would come. After many observations we knew the symptoms well, which made the correctness of our prognoses quite certain. "He won't last long," or, "This is the next one," we whispered to each other, and when, during our daily search for lice, we saw our own naked bodies in the evening, we thought alike: This body here, my body, is really a corpse already. What has become of me? I am but a small portion of a great mass of human flesh... of a mass behind barbed wire, crowded into a few earthen huts; a mass of which daily a certain portion begins to rot because it has become lifeless.

I mentioned above how unavoidable were the thoughts about food and favorite dishes which forced themselves into the consciousness of the prisoner, whenever he had a moment to spare. Perhaps it can be understood, then, that even the strongest of us was longing for the time when he would have fairly good food again, not for the sake of good food itself, but for the sake of knowing that the sub-human existence, which had made us unable to think of anything other than food, would at last cease.

Those who have not gone through a similar experience can hardly conceive of the soul-destroying mental conflict and clashes of will power which a famished man experiences. They can hardly grasp what it means to stand digging in a trench, listening only for the siren to announce 9:30 or 10:00 A.M.—the half-hour lunch interval—when bread would be rationed out (as long as it was still available); repeatedly asking the foreman—if he wasn't a disagreeable fellow—what the time was; and tenderly touching a piece of bread in one's coat pocket, first stroking it with frozen gloveless fingers, then breaking off a crumb and putting it in one's mouth and finally, with the last bit of will power, pocketing it again, having promised oneself that morning to hold out till afternoon.

We could hold endless debates on the sense or nonsense of certain methods of dealing with the small bread ration, which was given out only once daily during the latter part of our confinement. There were two schools of thought. One was in favor of eating up the ration immediately. This had the twofold advantage of satisfying the worst hunger pangs for a very short time at least once a day and of safeguarding against possible theft or loss of the ration. The second group, which held with dividing the ration up, used different arguments. I finally joined their ranks.

The most ghastly moment of the twenty-four hours of camp life was the awakening, when, at a still nocturnal hour, the three shrill blows of a whistle tore us pitilessly from our exhausted sleep and from the longings in our dreams. We then began the tussle with our wet shoes, into which we could scarcely force our feet, which were sore and swollen with edema. And there were the usual moans and groans about petty troubles, such as the snapping of wires which replaced shoelaces. One morning I heard someone, whom I knew to be brave and dignified, cry like a child because he finally had to go to the snowy marching grounds in his bare feet, as his shoes were too shrunken for him to wear. In those ghastly minutes, I found a little bit of comfort; a small piece of bread which I drew out of my pocket and munched with absorbed delight.

Undernourishment, besides being the cause of the general preoccupation with food, probably also explains the fact that the sexual urge was generally absent. Apart from the initial effects of shock, this appears to be the only explanation of a phenomenon which a psychologist was bound to observe in those all-male camps: that, as opposed to all other strictly male establishments—such as army barracks—there was little sexual perversion. Even in his dreams the prisoner did not seem to concern himself with sex, although his frustrated emotions and his finer, higher feelings did find definite expression in them.

With the majority of the prisoners, the primitive life and the effort of having to concentrate on just saving one's skin led to a total disregard of anything not serving that purpose, and explained the prisoners' complete lack of sentiment. This was brought home to me on my transfer from Auschwitz to a camp affiliated with Dachau. The train which carried us —about 2,000 prisoners—passed through Vienna. At about midnight we passed one of the Viennese railway stations. The track was going to lead us past the street where I was born, past the house where I had lived many years of my life, in fact, until I was taken prisoner.

There were fifty of us in the prison car, which had two small, barred peepholes. There was only enough room for one group to squat on the floor, while the others, who had to stand up for hours, crowded round the peepholes. Standing on tiptoe and looking past the others' heads through the bars of the window, I caught an eerie glimpse of my native town. We all felt more dead than alive, since we thought that our transport was heading for the camp at Mauthausen and that we had only one or two weeks to live. I had a distinct feeling that I saw the streets, the squares and the houses of my childhood with the eyes of a dead man who had come back from another world and was looking down on a ghostly city.

After hours of delay the train left the station. And there was the street—my street! The young lads who had a number of years of camp life behind them and for whom such a journey was a great event stared attentively through the peep-hole. I began to beg them, to entreat them, to let me stand in front for one moment only. I tried to explain how much a look through that window meant to me just then. My request was refused with rudeness and cynicism: "You lived here all those years? Well, then you have seen quite enough already!"

In general there was also a "cultural hibernation" in the camp. There were two exceptions to this: politics and religion. Politics were talked about everywhere in camp, almost continuously; the discussions were based chiefly on rumors, which were snapped up and passed around avidly. The rumors about the military situation were usually contradictory. They followed one another rapidly and succeeded only in making a contribution to the war of nerves that was waged in the minds of all the prisoners. Many times, hopes for a speedy end to the war, which had been fanned by optimistic rumors, were disappointed. Some men lost all hope, but it was the incorrigible optimists who were the most irritating companions.

The religious interest of the prisoners, as far and as soon as it developed, was the most sincere imaginable. The depth and vigor of religious belief often surprised and moved a new arrival. Most impressive in this connection were improvised prayers or services in the corner of a hut, or in the darkness of the locked cattle truck in which we were brought back from a distant work site, tired, hungry and frozen in our ragged clothing.

In the winter and spring of 1945 there was an outbreak of typhus which infected nearly all the prisoners. The mortality was great among the weak, who had to keep on with their hard work as long as they possibly could. The quarters for the sick were most inadequate, there were practically no medicines or attendants. Some of the symptoms of the disease were extremely disagreeable: an irrepressible aversion to even a scrap of food (which was an additional danger to life) and terrible attacks of delirium. The worst case of delirium was suffered by a friend of mine who thought that he was dying and wanted to pray. In his delirium he could not find the words to do so. To avoid these attacks of delirium, I tried, as did many of the others, to keep awake for most of the night. For hours I composed speeches in my mind. Eventually I began to reconstruct the manuscript which I had lost in the disinfection chamber of Auschwitz, and scribbled the key words in shorthand on tiny scraps of paper.

Occasionally a scientific debate developed in camp. Once I witnessed something I had never seen, even in my normal life, although it lay somewhat near my own professional interests: a spiritualistic seance. I had been invited to attend by the camp's chief doctor (also a prisoner), who knew that I was a specialist in psychiatry. The meeting took place in his small, private room in the sick quarters. A small circle had gathered, among them, quite illegally, the warrant officer from the sanitation squad.

One man began to invoke the spirits with a kind of prayer. The camp's clerk sat in front of a blank sheet of paper, without any conscious intention of writing. During the next ten minutes (after which time the seance was terminated because of the medium's failure to conjure the spirits to appear) his pencil slowly drew lines across the paper, forming quite legibly "VAE V." It was asserted that the clerk had never learned Latin and that he had never before heard the words "*vae victis*"—woe to the vanquished. In my opinion he must have heard them once in his life, without recollecting them, and they must have been available to the "spirit" (the spirit of his subconscious mind) at that time, a few months before our liberation and the end of the war.

In spite of all the enforced physical and mental primitiveness of the life in a concentration camp, it was possible for spiritual life to deepen. Sensitive people who were used to a rich intellectual life may have suffered much pain (they were often of a delicate constitution), but the damage to their inner selves was less. They were able to retreat from their terrible surroundings to a life of inner riches and spiritual freedom. Only in this way can one explain the apparent paradox that some prisoners of a less hardy make-up often seemed to survive camp life better than did those of a robust nature. In order to make myself clear, I am forced to fall back on personal experience. Let me tell what happened on those early mornings when we had to march to our work site.

There were shouted commands: "Detachment, forward march! Left-2-3-4! Left-2-3-4! Left-2-3-4! Left-2-3-4! First man about, left and left and left and left! Caps off!" These words sound in my ears even now. At the order "Caps off!" we passed the gate of the camp, and searchlights were trained upon us. Whoever did not march smartly got a kick. And worse off was the man who, because of the cold, had pulled his cap back over his ears before permission was given.

We stumbled on in the darkness, over big stones and through large puddles, along the one road leading from the camp. The accompanying guards kept shouting at us and driving us with the butts of their rifles. Anyone with very sore feet supported himself on his neighbor's arm. Hardly a word was spoken; the icy wind did not encourage talk. Hiding his mouth behind his upturned collar, the man marching next to me whispered suddenly: "If our wives could see us now! I do hope they are better off in their camps and don't know what is happening to us."

That brought thoughts of my own wife to mind. And as we stumbled on for miles, slipping on icy spots, supporting each other time and again, dragging one another up and onward, nothing was said, but we both knew: each of us was thinking of his wife. Occasionally I looked at the sky, where the stars were fading and the pink light of the morning was beginning to spread behind a dark bank of clouds. But my mind clung to my wife's image, imagining it with an uncanny acuteness. I heard her answering me, saw her smile, her frank and encouraging look. Real or not, her look was then more luminous than the sun which was beginning to rise.

A thought transfixed me: for the first time in my life I saw the truth as it is set into song by so many poets, proclaimed as the final wisdom by so many thinkers. The truth—that love is the ultimate and the highest goal to which man can aspire. Then I grasped the meaning of the greatest secret that human poetry and human thought and belief have to impart: *The salvation of man is through love and in love.* I understood how a man who has nothing left in this world still may know bliss, be it only for a brief moment, in the contemplation of his beloved. In a position of utter desolation, when man cannot express himself in positive action, when his only achievement may consist in enduring his sufferings in the right way —an honorable way—in such a position man can, through loving contemplation of the image he carries of his beloved, achieve fulfillment. For the first time in my life I was able to understand the meaning of the words, "The angels are lost in perpetual contemplation of an infinite glory."

In front of me a man stumbled and those following him fell on top of him. The guard rushed over and used his whip on them all. Thus my thoughts were interrupted for a few minutes. But soon my soul found its way back from the prisoner's existence to another world, and I resumed talk with my loved one: I asked her questions, and she answered; she questioned me in return, and I answered.

"Stop!" We had arrived at our work site. Everybody rushed into the dark hut in the hope of getting a fairly decent tool. Each prisoner got a spade or a pickaxe.

"Can't you hurry up, you pigs?" Soon we had resumed the previous day's positions in the ditch. The frozen ground cracked under the point of the pickaxes, and sparks flew. The men were silent, their brains numb.

My mind still clung to the image of my wife. A thought crossed my mind: I didn't even know if she were still alive. I knew only one thing—which I have learned well by now: Love goes very far beyond the physical person of the beloved. It finds its deepest meaning in his spiritual being, his inner self. Whether or not he is actually present, whether or not he is still alive at all, ceases somehow to be of importance.

I did not know whether my wife was alive, and I had no means of finding out (during all my prison life there was no outgoing or incoming mail); but at that moment it ceased to matter. There was no need for me to know; nothing could touch the strength of my love, my thoughts, and the image of my beloved. Had I known then that my wife was dead, I think that I would still have given myself, undisturbed by that knowledge, to the contemplation of her image, and that my mental conversation with her would have been just as vivid and just as satisfying. "Set me like a seal upon thy heart, love is as strong as death."

This intensification of inner life helped the prisoner find a refuge from the emptiness, desolation and spiritual poverty of his existence, by letting him escape into the past. When given free rein, his imagination played with past events, often not important ones, but minor happenings and trifling things. His nostalgic memory glorified them and they assumed a strange character. Their world and their existence seemed very distant and the spirit reached out for them longingly: In my mind I took bus rides, unlocked the front door of my apartment, answered my telephone, switched on the electric lights. Our thoughts often centered on such details, and these memories could move one to tears.

As the inner life of the prisoner tended to become more intense, he also experienced the beauty of art and nature as never before. Under their influence he sometimes even forgot his own frightful circumstances. If someone had seen our faces on the journey from Auschwitz to a Bavarian camp as we beheld the mountains of Salzburg with their summits glowing in the sunset, through the little barred windows of the prison carriage, he would never have believed that those were the faces of men who had given up all hope of life and liberty. Despite that factor—or maybe because of it—we were carried away by nature's beauty, which we had missed for so long.

In camp, too, a man might draw the attention of a comrade working next to him to a nice view of the setting sun shining through the tall trees of the Bavarian woods (as in the famous water color by Dürer), the same woods in which we had built an enormous, hidden munitions plant. One evening, when we were already resting on the floor of our hut, dead tired, soup bowls in hand, a fellow prisoner rushed in and asked us to run out to the assembly grounds and see the wonderful sunset. Standing outside we saw sinister clouds glowing in the west and the whole sky alive with clouds of ever-changing shapes and colors, from steel blue to blood red. The desolate grey mud huts provided a sharp contrast, while the puddles on the muddy ground reflected the glowing sky. Then, after minutes of moving silence, one prisoner said to another, "How beautiful the world *could* be!"

Another time we were at work in a trench. The dawn was grey around us; grey was the sky above; grey the snow in the pale light of dawn; grey the rags in which my fellow prisoners were clad, and grey their faces. I was again conversing silently with my wife, or perhaps I was struggling to find the *reason* for my sufferings, my slow dying. In a last violent protest against the hopelessness of imminent death, I sensed my spirit piercing through the enveloping gloom. I felt it transcend that hopeless, meaningless world, and from somewhere I heard a victorious "Yes" in answer to my question of the existence of an ultimate purpose. At that moment a light was lit in a distant farmhouse, which stood on the horizon as if painted there, in the midst of the miserable grey of a dawning morning in Bavaria. *"Et lux in tenebris lucet"*—and the light shineth in the darkness. For hours I stood hacking at the icy ground. The guard passed by, insulting me, and once again I communed with my beloved. More and more I felt that she was present, that she was with me; I had the feeling that I was able to touch her, able to stretch out my hand and grasp hers. The feeling was very strong: she was *there*. Then, at that very moment, a bird flew down silently and perched just in front of me, on the heap of soil which I had dug up from the ditch, and looked steadily at me.

Earlier, I mentioned art. Is there such a thing in a concentration camp? It rather depends on what one chooses to call art. A kind of cabaret was improvised from time to time. A hut was cleared temporarily, a few wooden benches were pushed or nailed together and a program was drawn up. In the evening those who had fairly good positions in camp—the Capos and the workers who did not have to leave camp on distant marches—assembled there. They came to have a few laughs or perhaps to cry a little; anyway, to forget. There were songs, poems, jokes, some with underlying satire regarding the camp. All were meant to help us forget, and they did help. The gatherings were so effective that a few ordinary prisoners went to see the cabaret in spite of their fatigue even though they missed their daily portion of food by going.

During the half-hour lunch interval when soup (which the contractors paid for and for which they did not spend much) was ladled out at our work site, we were allowed to assemble in an unfinished engine room. On entering, everyone got a ladleful of the watery soup. While we sipped it greedily, a prisoner climbed onto a tub and sang Italian arias. We enjoyed the songs, and he was guaranteed a double helping of soup, straight "from the bottom"—that meant with peas!

Rewards were given in camp not only for entertainment, but also for applause. I, for example, could have found protection (how lucky I was never in need of it!) from the camp's most dreaded Capo, who for more than one good reason was known as "The Murderous Capo." This is how it happened. One evening I had the great honor of being invited again to the room where the spiritualistic seance had taken place. There were gathered the same intimate friends of the chief doctor and, most illegally, the warrant officer from the sanitation squad was again present. The Murderous Capo entered the room by chance, and he was asked to recite one of his poems, which had become famous (or infamous) in camp. He did not need to be asked twice and quickly produced a kind of diary from which he began to read samples of his art. I bit my lips till they hurt in order to keep from laughing at one of his love poems, and very likely that saved my life. Since I was also generous with my applause, my life might have been saved even had I been detailed to his working party to which I had previously been assigned for one day—a day that was quite enough for me. It was useful, anyway, to be known to The Murderous Capo from a favorable angle. So I applauded as hard as I could.

Generally speaking, of course, any pursuit of art in camp was somewhat grotesque. I would say that the real impression made by anything connected with art arose only from the ghostlike contrast between the performance and the background of desolate camp life. I shall never forget how I awoke from the deep sleep of exhaustion on my second night in Auschwitz—roused by music. The senior warden of the hut had some kind of celebration in his room, which was near the entrance of the hut. Tipsy voices bawled some hackneyed tunes. Suddenly there was a silence and into the night a violin sang a desperately sad tango, an unusual tune not spoiled by frequent playing. The violin wept and a part of me wept with it, for on that same day someone had a twenty-fourth birthday. That someone lay in another part of the Auschwitz camp, possibly only a few hundred or a thousand yards away, and yet completely out of reach. That someone was my wife.

To discover that there was any semblance of art in a concentration camp must be surprise enough for an outsider, but he may be even more astonished to hear that one could find a sense of humor there as well; of course, only the faint trace of one, and then only for a few seconds or minutes. Humor was another of the soul's weapons in the fight for self-preservation. It is well known that humor, more than anything else in the human make-up, can afford an aloofness and an ability to rise above any situation, even if only for a few seconds. I practically trained a friend of mine who worked next to me on the building site to develop a sense of humor. I suggested to him that we would promise each other to invent at least one amusing story daily, about some incident that could happen one day after our liberation. He was a surgeon and had been an assistant on the staff of a large hospital. So I once tried to get him to smile by describing to him how he would be unable to lose the habits of camp life when he returned to his former work. On the building site (especially when the supervisor made his tour of inspection) the foreman encouraged us to work faster by shouting: "Action! Action!" I told my friend, "One day you will be back in the operating room, performing a big abdominal operation. Suddenly an orderly will rush in announcing the arrival of the senior surgeon by shouting, 'Action! Action!' "

Sometimes the other men invented amusing dreams about the future, such as forecasting that during a future dinner engagement they might forget themselves when the soup was served and beg the hostess to ladle it "from the bottom."

The attempt to develop a sense of humor and to see things in a humorous light is some kind of a trick learned while mastering the art of living. Yet it is possible to practice the art of living even in a concentration camp, although suffering is omnipresent. To draw an analogy: a man's suffering is similar to the behavior of gas. If a certain quantity of gas is pumped into an empty chamber, it will fill the chamber completely and evenly, no matter how big the chamber. Thus suffering completely fills the human soul and conscious mind, no matter whether the suffering is great or little. Therefore the "size" of human suffering is absolutely relative.

It also follows that a very trifling thing can cause the greatest of joys. Take as an example something that happened on our journey from Auschwitz to the camp affiliated with Dachau. We had all been afraid that our transport was heading for the Mauthausen camp. We became more and more tense as we approached a certain bridge over the Danube which the train would have to cross to reach Mauthausen, according to the statement of experienced traveling companions. Those who have never seen anything similar cannot possibly imagine the dance of joy performed in the carriage by the prisoners when they saw that our transport was not crossing the bridge and was instead heading "only" for Dachau.*

And again, what happened on our arrival in that camp, after a journey lasting two days and three nights? There had not been enough room for everybody to crouch on the floor of the carriage at the same time. The majority of us had to stand all the way, while a few took turns at squatting on the scanty straw which was soaked with human urine. When we arrived the first important news that we heard from older prisoners was that this comparatively small camp (its population was 2,500) had no "oven," no crematorium, no gas! That meant that a person who had become a "Moslem" could not be taken straight to the gas chamber, but would have to wait until a so-called "sick convoy" had been arranged to return to Auschwitz. This joyful surprise put us all in a good mood. The wish of the senior warden of our hut in Auschwitz had come true: we had come, as quickly as possible, to a camp which did not have a "chimney"—unlike Auschwitz. We laughed and cracked jokes in spite of, and during, all we had to go through in the next few hours.

When we new arrivals were counted, one of us was missing. So we had to wait outside in the rain and cold wind until the missing man was found. He was at last discovered in a hut, where he had fallen asleep from exhaustion. Then the roll call was turned into a punishment parade. All through the night and late into the next morning, we had to stand outside, frozen and soaked to the skin after the strain of our long journey. And yet we were all very pleased! There was no chimney in this camp and Auschwitz was a long way off.

Another time we saw a group of convicts pass our work site. How obvious the relativity of all suffering appeared to us then! We envied those prisoners their relatively well-regulated, secure and happy life. They surely had regular opportunities to take baths, we thought sadly. They surely had toothbrushes and clothesbrushes, mattresses—a separate one for each of them—and monthly mail bringing them news of the whereabouts of their relatives, or at least of whether they were still alive or not. We had lost all that a long time ago.

And how we envied those of us who had the opportunity to get into a factory and work in a sheltered room! It was everyone's wish to have such a lifesaving piece of luck. The scale of relative luck extends even further. Even among those detachments outside the camp (in one of which I was a member) there were some units which were considered worse than others. One could envy a man who did not have to wade in deep, muddy clay on a steep slope emptying the tubs of a small field railway for twelve hours daily. Most of the daily accidents occurred on this job, and they were often fatal.

In other work parties the foremen maintained an apparently local tradition of dealing out numerous blows, which made us talk of the relative luck of not being under their command, or perhaps of being under it only temporarily. Once, by an unlucky chance, I got into such a group. If an air raid alarm had not interrupted us after two hours (during which time the foreman had worked on me especially), making it necessary to regroup the workers afterwards, I think that I would have returned to camp on one of the sledges which carried those who had died or were dying from exhaustion. No one can imagine the relief that the siren can bring in such a situation; not even a boxer who has heard the bell signifying the finish of a round and who is thus saved at the last minute from the danger of a knockout.

We were grateful for the smallest of mercies. We were glad when there was time to delouse before going to bed, although in itself this was no pleasure, as it meant standing naked in an unheated hut where icicles hung from the ceiling. But we were thankful if there was no air raid alarm during this operation and the lights were not switched off. If we could not do the job properly, we were kept awake half the night.

The meager pleasures of camp life provided a kind of negative happiness—"freedom from suffering" as Schopenhauer put it—and even that in a relative way only. Real positive pleasures, even small ones, were very few. I remember drawing up a kind of balance sheet of pleasures one day and finding that in many, many past weeks I had experienced only two pleasurable moments. One occurred when, on returning from work, I was admitted to the cook house after a long wait and was assigned to the line filing up to prisoner-cook F——. He stood behind one of the huge pans and ladled soup into the bowls which were held out to him by the prisoners, who hurriedly filed past. He was the only cook who did not look at the men whose bowls he was filling; the only cook who dealt out the soup equally, regardless of recipient, and who did not make favorites of his personal friends or countrymen, picking out the potatoes for them, while the others got watery soup skimmed from the top.

But it is not for me to pass judgment on those prisoners who put their own people above everyone else. Who can throw a stone at a man who favors his friends under circumstances when, sooner or later, it is a question of life or death? No man should judge unless he asks himself in absolute honesty whether in a similar situation he might not have done the same.

Long after I had resumed normal life again (that means a long time after my release from camp), somebody showed me an illustrated weekly with photographs of prisoners lying crowded on their bunks, staring dully at a visitor. "Isn't this terrible, the dreadful staring faces—everything about it."

"Why?" I asked, for I genuinely did not understand. For at that moment I saw it all again: at 5:00 A.M. it was still pitch dark outside. I was lying on the hard boards in an earthen hut where about seventy of us were "taken care of." We were sick and did not have to leave camp for work; we did not have to go on parade. We could lie all day in our little corner in the hut and doze and wait for the daily distribution of bread (which, of course, was reduced for the sick) and for the daily helping of soup (watered down and also decreased in quantity). But how content we were; happy in spite of everything. While we cowered against each other to avoid any unnecessary loss of warmth, and were too lazy and disinterested to move a finger unnecessarily, we heard shrill whistles and shouts from the square where the night shift had just returned and was assembling for roll call. The door was flung open, and the snowstorm blew into our hut. An exhausted comrade, covered with snow, stumbled inside to sit down for a few minutes. But the senior warden turned him out again. It was strictly forbidden to admit a stranger to a hut while a check-up on the men was in progress. How sorry I was for that fellow and how glad not to be in his skin at that moment, but instead to be sick and able to doze on in the sick quarters! What a lifesaver it was to have two days there, and perhaps even two extra days after those!

All this came to my mind when I saw the photographs in the magazine. When I explained, my listeners understood why I did not find the photograph so terrible: the people shown on it might not have been so unhappy after all.

On my fourth day in the sick quarters I had just been detailed to the night shift when the chief doctor rushed in and asked me to volunteer for medical duties in another camp containing typhus patients. Against the urgent advice of my friends (and despite the fact that almost none of my colleagues offered their services), I decided to volunteer. I knew that in a working party I would die in a short time. But if I had to die there might at least be some sense in my death. I thought that it would doubtless be more to the purpose to try and help my comrades as a doctor than to vegetate or finally lose my life as the unproductive laborer that I was then.

For me this was simple mathematics, not sacrifice. But secretly, the warrant officer from the sanitation squad had ordered that the two doctors who had volunteered for the typhus camp should be "taken care of" till they left. We looked so weak that he feared that he might have two additional corpses on his hands, rather than two doctors.

I mentioned earlier how everything that was not connected with the immediate task of keeping oneself and one's closest friends alive lost its value. Everything was sacrificed to this end. A man's character became involved to the point that he was caught in a mental turmoil which threatened all the values he held and threw them into doubt. Under the influence of a world which no longer recognized the value of human life and human dignity, which had robbed man of his will and had made him an object to be exterminated (having planned, however, to make full use of him first—to the last ounce of his physical resources)—under this influence the personal ego finally suffered a loss of values. If the man in the concentration camp did not struggle against this in a last effort to save his self-respect, he lost the feeling of being an individual, a being with a mind, with inner freedom and personal value. He thought of himself then as only a part of an enormous mass of people; his existence descended to the level of animal life. The men were herded—sometimes to one place then to another; sometimes driven together, then apart—like a flock of sheep without a thought or a will of their own. A small but dangerous pack watched them from all sides, well versed in methods of torture and sadism. They drove the herd incessantly, backwards and forwards, with shouts, kicks and blows. And we, the sheep, thought of two things only—how to evade the bad dogs and how to get a little food.

Just like sheep that crowd timidly into the center of a herd, each of us tried to get into the middle of our formations. That gave one a better chance of avoiding the blows of the guards who were marching on either side and to the front and rear of our column. The central position had the added advantage of affording protection against the bitter winds. It was, therefore, in an attempt to save one's own skin that one literally tried to submerge into the crowd. This was done automati-

cally in the formations. But at other times it was a very conscious effort on our part—in conformity with one of the
camp's most imperative laws of self-preservation: Do not be
conspicuous. We tried at all times to avoid attracting the attention of the SS.

There were times, of course, when it was possible, and
even necessary, to keep away from the crowd. It is well known
that an enforced community life, in which attention is paid to
everything one does at all times, may result in an irresistible
urge to get away, at least for a short while. The prisoner craved
to be alone with himself and his thoughts. He yearned for pri-
vacy and for solitude. After my transportation to a so-called
"rest camp," I had the rare fortune to find solitude for about
five minutes at a time. Behind the earthen hut where I worked
and in which were crowded about fifty delirious patients,
there was a quiet spot in a corner of the double fence of
barbed wire surrounding the camp. A tent had been improvised there with a few poles and branches of trees in order
to shelter a half-dozen corpses (the daily death rate in the
camp). There was also a shaft leading to the water pipes. I
squatted on the wooden lid of this shaft whenever my services were not needed. I just sat and looked out at the green
flowering slopes and the distant blue hills of the Bavarian
landscape, framed by the meshes of barbed wire. I dreamed
longingly, and my thoughts wandered north and northeast,
in the direction of my home, but I could only see clouds.

The corpses near me, crawling with lice, did not bother
me. Only the steps of passing guards could rouse me from
my dreams; or perhaps it would be a call to the sick-bay or to
collect a newly arrived supply of medicine for my hut—con-

sisting of perhaps five or ten tablets of aspirin, to last for several days for fifty patients. I collected them and then did my rounds, feeling the patients' pulses and giving half-tablets to the serious cases. But the desperately ill received no medicine. It would not have helped, and besides, it would have deprived those for whom there was still some hope. For light cases, I had nothing, except perhaps a word of encouragement. In this way I dragged myself from patient to patient, though I myself was weak and exhausted from a serious attack of typhus. Then I went back to my lonely place on the wood cover of the water shaft.

This shaft, incidentally, once saved the lives of three fellow prisoners. Shortly before liberation, mass transports were organized to go to Dachau, and these three prisoners wisely tried to avoid the trip. They climbed down the shaft and hid there from the guards. I calmly sat on the lid, looking innocent and playing a childish game of throwing pebbles at the barbed wire. On spotting me, the guard hesitated for a moment, but then passed on. Soon I could tell the three men below that the worst danger was over.

It is very difficult for an outsider to grasp how very little value was placed on human life in camp. The camp inmate was hardened, but possibly became more conscious of this complete disregard of human existence when a convoy of sick men was arranged. The emaciated bodies of the sick were thrown on two-wheeled carts which were drawn by prisoners for many miles, often through snowstorms, to the next camp. If one of the sick men had died before the cart left, he was thrown on anyway—the list had to be correct! The list was the only thing that mattered. A man counted only because he had a prison number. One literally became a number: dead or alive—that was unimportant; the life of a "number" was completely irrelevant. What stood behind that number and that life mattered even less: the fate, the history, the name of the man. In the transport of sick patients that I, in my capacity as a doctor, had to accompany from one camp in Bavaria to another, there was a young prisoner whose brother was not on the list and therefore would have to be left behind. The young man begged so long that the camp warden decided to work an exchange, and the brother took the place of a man who, at the moment, preferred to stay behind. But the list had to be correct! That was easy. The brother just exchanged numbers with the other prisoner.

As I have mentioned before, we had no documents; everyone was lucky to own his body, which, after all, was still breathing. All else about us, i.e., the rags hanging from our gaunt skeletons, was only of interest if we were assigned to a transport of sick patients. The departing "Moslems" were examined with unabashed curiosity to see whether their coats or shoes were not better than one's own. After all, their fates were sealed. But those who stayed behind in camp, who were still capable of some work, had to make use of every means to improve their chances of survival. They were not sentimental. The prisoners saw themselves completely dependent on the moods of the guards—playthings of fate—and this made them even less human than the circumstances warranted.

In Auschwitz I had laid down a rule for myself which proved to be a good one and which most of my comrades later followed. I generally answered all kinds of questions truthfully. But I was silent about anything that was not expressly asked for. If I were asked my age, I gave it. If asked about my profession, I said "doctor," but did not elaborate. The first morning in Auschwitz an SS officer came to the parade ground. We had to fall into separate groups of prisoners: over forty years, under forty years, metal workers, mechanics, and so forth. Then we were examined for ruptures and some prisoners had to form a new group. The group that I was in was driven to another hut, where we lined up again. After being sorted out once more and having answered questions as to my age and profession, I was sent to another small group. Once more we were driven to another hut and grouped differently. This continued for some time, and I became quite unhappy, finding myself among strangers who spoke unintelligible foreign languages. Then came the last selection, and I found myself back in the group that had been with me in the first hut! They had barely noticed that I had been sent from hut to hut in the meantime. But I was aware that in those few minutes fate had passed me in many different forms.

When the transport of sick patients for the "rest camp" was organized, my name (that is, my number) was put on the list, since a few doctors were needed. But no one was convinced that the destination was really a rest camp. A few weeks previously the same transport had been prepared. Then, too, everyone had thought that it was destined for the gas ovens. When it was announced that anyone who volunteered for the dreaded night shift would be taken off the transport list, eighty-two prisoners volunteered immediately. A quarter of an hour later the transport was canceled, but the eighty-two stayed on the list for the night shift. For the majority of them, this meant death within the next fortnight.

Now the transport for the rest camp was arranged for the second time. Again no one knew whether this was a ruse to obtain the last bit of work from the sick—if only for fourteen days—or whether it would go to the gas ovens or to a genuine rest camp. The chief doctor, who had taken a liking to me, told me furtively one evening at a quarter to ten, "I have made it known in the orderly room that you can still have your name crossed off the list; you may do so up till ten o'clock."

I told him that this was not my way; that I had learned to let fate take its course. "I might as well stay with my friends," I said. There was a look of pity in his eyes, as if he knew.... He shook my hand silently, as though it were a farewell, not for life, but from life. Slowly I walked back to my hut. There I found a good friend waiting for me.

"You really want to go with them?" he asked sadly.

"Yes, I am going."

Tears came to his eyes and I tried to comfort him. Then there was something else to do—to make my will:

"Listen, Otto, if I don't get back home to my wife, and if you should see her again, then tell her that I talked of her daily, hourly. You remember. Secondly, I have loved her more than anyone. Thirdly, the short time I have been married to her outweighs everything, even all we have gone through here."

Otto, where are you now? Are you alive? What has happened to you since our last hour together? Did you find your wife again? And do you remember how I made you learn my will by heart—word for word—in spite of your childlike tears?

The next morning I departed with the transport. This time

it was not a ruse. We were not heading for the gas chambers, and we actually did go to a rest camp. Those who had pitied me remained in a camp where famine was to rage even more fiercely than in our new camp. They tried to save themselves, but they only sealed their own fates. Months later, after liberation, I met a friend from the old camp. He related to me how he, as camp policeman, had searched for a piece of human flesh that was missing from a pile of corpses. He confiscated it from a pot in which he found it cooking. Cannibalism had broken out. I had left just in time.

Does this not bring to mind the story of Death in Teheran? A rich and mighty Persian once walked in his garden with one of his servants. The servant cried that he had just encountered Death, who had threatened him. He begged his master to give him his fastest horse so that he could make haste and flee to Teheran, which he could reach that same evening. The master consented and the servant galloped off on the horse. On returning to his house the master himself met Death, and questioned him, "Why did you terrify and threaten my servant?" "I did not threaten him; I only showed surprise in still finding him here when I planned to meet him tonight in Teheran," said Death.

The camp inmate was frightened of making decisions and of taking any sort of initiative whatsoever. This was the result of a strong feeling that fate was one's master, and that one must not try to influence it in any way, but instead let it take its own course. In addition, there was a great apathy, which contributed in no small part to the feelings of the prisoner. At times, lightning decisions had to be made, decisions which spelled life or death. The prisoner would have preferred to let fate make the choice for him. This escape from commitment was most apparent when a prisoner had to make the decision for or against an escape attempt. In those minutes in which he had to make up his mind—and it was always a question of minutes—he suffered the tortures of Hell. Should he make the attempt to flee? Should he take the risk?

I, too, experienced this torment. As the battle-front drew nearer, I had the opportunity to escape. A colleague of mine who had to visit huts outside the camp in the course of his medical duties wanted to escape and take me with him. Under the pretense of holding a consultation about a patient whose illness required a specialist's advice, he smuggled me out. Outside the camp, a member of a foreign resistance movement was to supply us with uniforms and documents. At the last moment there were some technical difficulties and we had to return to camp once more. We used this opportunity to provide ourselves with provisions—a few rotten potatoes—and to look for a rucksack.

We broke into an empty hut of the women's camp, which was vacant, as the women had been sent to another camp. The hut was in great disorder; it was obvious that many women had acquired supplies and fled. There were rags, straw, rotting food, and broken crockery. Some bowls were still in good condition and would have been very valuable to us, but we decided not to take them. We knew that lately, as conditions had become desperate, they had been used not only for food, but also as washbasins and chamber pots. (There was a strictly enforced rule against having any kind of utensil in the hut. However, some people were forced to break this rule, especially the typhus patients, who were much too weak to go outside even with help.) While I acted as a screen, my friend broke into the hut and returned shortly with a rucksack which he hid under his coat. He had seen another one inside which I was to take. So we changed places and I went in. As I searched in the rubbish, finding the rucksack and even a toothbrush, I suddenly saw, among all the things that had been left behind, the body of a woman.

I ran back to my hut to collect all my possessions: my food bowl, a pair of torn mittens "inherited" from a dead typhus patient, and a few scraps of paper covered with shorthand notes (on which, as I mentioned before, I had started to reconstruct the manuscript which I lost at Auschwitz). I made a quick last round of my patients, who were lying huddled on the rotten planks of wood on either side of the huts. I came to my only countryman, who was almost dying, and whose life it had been my ambition to save in spite of his condition. I had to keep my intention to escape to myself, but my comrade seemed to guess that something was wrong (perhaps I showed a little nervousness). In a tired voice he asked me, "You, too, are getting out?" I denied it, but I found it difficult to avoid his sad look. After my round I returned to him. Again a hopeless look greeted me and somehow I felt it to be an accusation. The unpleasant feeling that had gripped me as soon as I had told my friend I would escape with him became more intense. Suddenly I decided to take fate into my own hands for once. I ran out of the hut and told my friend that I could not go with him. As soon as I had told him with finality that I had made up my mind to stay with my patients, the unhappy feeling left me. I did not know what the following days would bring, but I had gained an inward peace that I had never experienced before. I returned to the hut, sat down on the boards at my countryman's feet and tried to comfort him; then I chatted with the others, trying to quiet them in their delirium.

Our last day in camp arrived. As the battle-front came nearer, mass transports had taken nearly all the prisoners to other camps. The camp authorities, the Capos and the cooks had fled. On this day an order was given that the camp must be evacuated completely by sunset. Even the few remaining prisoners (the sick, a few doctors, and some "nurses") would have to leave. At night, the camp was to be set on fire. In the afternoon the trucks which were to collect the sick had not yet appeared. Instead the camp gates were suddenly closed and the barbed wire closely watched, so that no one could attempt an escape. The remaining prisoners seemed to be destined to burn with the camp. For the second time my friend and I decided to escape.

We had been given an order to bury three men outside the barbed wire fence. We were the only two in camp who had strength enough to do the job. Nearly all the others lay in the few huts which were still in use, prostrate with fever and delirium. We now made our plans: along with the first body we would smuggle out my friend's rucksack, hiding it in the old laundry tub which served as a coffin. When we took out the second body we would also carry out my rucksack, and on the third trip we intended to make our escape. The first two trips went according to plan. After we returned, I waited while my friend tried to find a piece of bread so that we would have something to eat during the next few days in the woods.

I waited. Minutes passed. I became more and more impatient as he did not return. After three years of imprisonment, I was picturing freedom joyously, imagining how wonderful it would be to run toward the battle-front. But we did not get that far.

The very moment when my friend came back, the camp gate was thrown open. A splendid, aluminum-colored car, on which were painted large red crosses, slowly rolled on to the parade ground. A delegate from the International Red Cross in Geneva had arrived, and the camp and its inmates were under his protection. The delegate billeted himself in a farmhouse in the vicinity, in order to be near the camp at all times in case of emergency. Who worried about escape now? Boxes with medicines were unloaded from the car, cigarettes were distributed, we were photographed and joy reigned supreme. Now there was no need for us to risk running toward the fighting line.

In our excitement we had forgotten the third body, so we carried it outside and dropped it into the narrow grave we had dug for the three corpses. The guard who accompanied us— a relatively inoffensive man—suddenly became quite gentle. He saw that the tables might be turned and tried to win our goodwill. He joined in the short prayers that we offered for the dead men before throwing soil over them. After the tension and excitement of the past days and hours, those last days in our race with death, the words of our prayer asking for peace, were as fervent as any ever uttered by the human voice.

And so the last day in camp passed in anticipation of freedom. But we had rejoiced too early. The Red Cross delegate had assured us that an agreement had been signed, and that the camp must not be evacuated. But that night the SS arrived with trucks and brought an order to clear the camp. The last remaining prisoners were to be taken to a central camp, from which they would be sent to Switzerland within forty-eight hours—to be exchanged for some prisoners of war. We scarcely recognized the SS. They were so friendly, trying to persuade us to get in the trucks without fear, telling us that we should be grateful for our good luck. Those who were strong enough crowded into the trucks and the seriously ill and feeble were lifted up with difficulty. My friend and I—we did not hide our rucksacks now—stood in the last group, from which thirteen would be chosen for the next to last truck. The chief doctor counted out the requisite number, but he omitted the two of us. The thirteen were loaded into the truck and we had to stay behind. Surprised, very annoyed and disappointed, we blamed the chief doctor, who excused himself by saying that he had been tired and distracted. He said that he had thought we still intended to escape. Impatiently we sat down, keeping our rucksacks on our backs, and waited with the few remaining prisoners for the last truck. We had to wait a long time. Finally we lay down on the mattresses of the deserted guard-room, exhausted by the excitement of the last few hours and days, during which we had fluctuated continually between hope and despair. We slept in our clothes and shoes, ready for the journey.

The noise of rifles and cannons woke us; the flashes of tracer bullets and gun shots entered the hut. The chief doctor dashed in and ordered us to take cover on the floor. One prisoner jumped on my stomach from the bed above me and with his shoes on. That awakened me all right! Then we grasped what was happening: the battle-front had reached us! The shooting decreased and morning dawned. Outside on the pole at the camp gate a white flag floated in the wind.

Many weeks later we found out that even in those last hours fate had toyed with us few remaining prisoners. We found out just how uncertain human decisions are, especially in matters of life and death. I was confronted with photographs which had been taken in a small camp not far from ours. Our friends who had thought they were traveling to freedom that night had been taken in the trucks to this camp, and there they were locked in the huts and burned to death. Their partially charred bodies were recognizable on the photograph. I thought again of Death in Teheran.

Apart from its role as a defensive mechanism, the prisoners' apathy was also the result of other factors. Hunger and lack of sleep contributed to it (as they do in normal life, also) and to the general irritability which was another characteristic of the prisoners' mental state. The lack of sleep was due partly to the pestering of vermin which infested the terribly over-crowded huts because of the general lack of hygiene and sanitation. The fact that we had neither nicotine nor caffeine also contributed to the state of apathy and irritability.

Besides these physical causes, there were mental ones, in the form of certain complexes. The majority of prisoners suffered from a kind of inferiority complex. We all had once been or had fancied ourselves to be "somebody." Now we were treated like complete nonentities. (The consciousness of one's inner value is anchored in higher, more spiritual things, and cannot be shaken by camp life. But how many free men, let alone prisoners, possess it?) Without consciously thinking about it, the average prisoner felt himself utterly degraded. This became obvious when one observed the contrasts offered by the singular sociological structure of the camp. The more "prominent" prisoners, the Capos, the cooks, the store-keepers and the camp policemen, did not, as a rule, feel degraded at all, like the majority of prisoners, but on the contrary—promoted! Some even developed miniature delusions of grandeur. The mental reaction of the envious and grumbling majority toward this favored minority found expression in several ways, sometimes in jokes. For instance, I heard one prisoner talk to another about a Capo, saying, "Imagine! I knew that man when he was only the president of a large bank. Isn't it fortunate that he has risen so far in the world?"

Whenever the degraded majority and the promoted minority came into conflict (and there were plenty of opportunities for this, starting with the distribution of food) the results were explosive. Therefore, the general irritability (whose physical causes were discussed above) became most intense when these mental tensions were added. It is not surprising that this tension often ended in a general fight. Since the prisoner continually witnessed scenes of beatings, the impulse toward violence was increased. I myself felt my fists clench when anger came over me while I was famished and tired. I was usually very tired, since we had to stoke our stove—which we were allowed to keep in our hut for the typhus patients—throughout the nights. However, some of the most idyllic hours I have ever spent were in the middle of the night when all the others were delirious or sleeping. I could lie stretched out in front of the stove and roast a few pilfered potatoes in a fire made from stolen charcoal. But the following day I always felt even more tired, insensitive and irritable.

While I was working as a doctor in the typhus block, I also had to take the place of the senior block warden who was ill. Therefore, I was responsible to the camp authority for keeping the hut clean—if "clean" can be used to describe such a condition. The pretense at inspection to which the hut was frequently submitted was more for the purpose of torture than of hygiene. More food and a few drugs would have helped, but the only concern of the inspectors was whether a piece of straw was left in the center corridor, or whether the dirty, ragged and verminous blankets of the patients were tucked in neatly at their feet. As to the fate of the inmates, they were quite unconcerned. If I reported smartly, whipping my prison cap from my shorn head and clicking my heels, "Hut number VI/9: 52 patients, two nursing orderlies, and one doctor," they were satisfied. And then they would leave. But until they arrived—often they were hours later than announced, and sometimes did not come at all—I was forced to keep straightening blankets, picking up bits of straw which fell from the bunks, and shouting at the poor devils who tossed in their beds and threatened to upset all my efforts at tidiness and cleanliness. Apathy was particularly increased among the feverish patients, so that they did not react at all unless they were shouted at. Even this failed at times, and then it took tremendous self-control not to strike them. For one's own irritability took on enormous proportions in the face of the other's apathy and especially in the face of the danger (i.e., the approaching inspection) which was caused by it.

In attempting this psychological presentation and a psychopathological explanation of the typical characteristics of a concentration camp inmate, I may give the impression that the human being is completely and unavoidably influenced by his surroundings. (In this case the surroundings being the unique structure of camp life, which forced the prisoner to conform his conduct to a certain set pattern.) But what about human liberty? Is there no spiritual freedom in regard to behavior and reaction to any given surroundings? Is that theory true which would have us believe that man is no more than a product of many conditional and environmental factors—be they of a biological, psychological or sociological nature? Is man but an accidental product of these? Most important, do the prisoners' reactions to the singular world of the concentration camp prove that man cannot escape the influences of his surroundings? Does man have no choice of action in the face of such circumstances?

We can answer these questions from experience as well as on principle. The experiences of camp life show that man does have a choice of action. There were enough examples, often of a heroic nature, which proved that apathy could be overcome, irritability suppressed. Man *can* preserve a vestige of spiritual freedom, of independence of mind, even in such terrible conditions of psychic and physical stress.

We who lived in concentration camps can remember the men who walked through the huts comforting others, giving away their last piece of bread. They may have been few in number, but they offer sufficient proof that everything can be taken from a man but one thing: the last of the human freedoms—to choose one's attitude in any given set of circumstances, to choose one's own way.

And there were always choices to make. Every day, every hour, offered the opportunity to make a decision, a decision which determined whether you would or would not submit to those powers which threatened to rob you of your very self, your inner freedom; which determined whether or not you would become the plaything of circumstance, renouncing freedom and dignity to become molded into the form of the typical inmate.

Seen from this point of view, the mental reactions of the inmates of a concentration camp must seem more to us than the mere expression of certain physical and sociological conditions. Even though conditions such as lack of sleep, insufficient food and various mental stresses may suggest that the inmates were bound to react in certain ways, in the final analysis it becomes clear that the sort of person the prisoner became was the result of an inner decision, and not the result of camp influences alone. Fundamentally, therefore, any man can, even under such circumstances, decide what shall become of him—mentally and spiritually. He may retain his human dignity even in a concentration camp. Dostoevski said once, "There is only one thing that I dread: not to be worthy of my sufferings." These words frequently came to my mind after I became acquainted with those martyrs whose behavior in camp, whose suffering and death, bore witness to the fact that the last inner freedom cannot be lost. It can be said that they were worthy of their sufferings; the way they bore their suffering was a genuine inner achievement. It is this spiritual freedom—which cannot be taken away—that makes life meaningful and purposeful.

An active life serves the purpose of giving man the opportunity to realize values in creative work, while a passive life of enjoyment affords him the opportunity to obtain fulfillment in experiencing beauty, art, or nature. But there is also purpose in that life which is almost barren of both creation and enjoyment and which admits of but one possibility of high moral behavior: namely, in man's attitude to his existence, an existence restricted by external forces. A creative life and a life of enjoyment are banned to him. But not only creativeness and enjoyment are meaningful. If there is a meaning in life at all, then there must be a meaning in suffering. Suffering is an ineradicable part of life, even as fate and death. Without suffering and death human life cannot be complete.

The way in which a man accepts his fate and all the suffering it entails, the way in which he takes up his cross, gives him ample opportunity—even under the most difficult circumstances—to add a deeper meaning to his life. It may remain brave, dignified and unselfish. Or in the bitter fight for self-preservation he may forget his human dignity and become no more than an animal. Here lies the chance for a man either to make use of or to forgo the opportunities of attaining the moral values that a difficult situation may afford him. And this decides whether he is worthy of his sufferings or not.

Do not think that these considerations are unworldly and too far removed from real life. It is true that only a few people are capable of reaching such high moral standards. Of the prisoners only a few kept their full inner liberty and obtained those values which their suffering afforded, but even one such example is sufficient proof that man's inner strength may raise him above his outward fate. Such men are not only in concentration camps. Everywhere man is confronted with fate, with the chance of achieving something through his own suffering.

Take the fate of the sick—especially those who are incurable. I once read a letter written by a young invalid, in which he told a friend that he had just found out he would not live for long, that even an operation would be of no help. He wrote further that he remembered a film he had seen in which a man was portrayed who waited for death in a courageous and dignified way. The boy had thought it a great accomplishment to meet death so well. Now—he wrote—fate was offering him a similar chance.

Those of us who saw the film called *Resurrection*—taken from a book by Tolstoy—years ago, may have had similar thoughts. Here were great destinies and great men. For us, at that time, there was no great fate; there was no chance to achieve such greatness. After the picture we went to the nearest café, and over a cup of coffee and a sandwich we forgot the strange metaphysical thoughts which for one moment had crossed our minds. But when we ourselves were confronted with a great destiny and faced with the decision of meeting it with equal spiritual greatness, by then we had forgotten our youthful resolutions of long ago, and we failed.

Perhaps there came a day for some of us when we saw the same film again, or a similar one. But by then other pictures may have simultaneously unrolled before one's inner eye; pictures of people who attained much more in their lives than a sentimental film could show. Some details of a particular man's inner greatness may have come to one's mind, like the story of the young woman whose death I witnessed in a concentration camp. It is a simple story. There is little to tell and it may sound as if I had invented it; but to me it seems like a poem.

This young woman knew that she would die in the next few days. But when I talked to her she was cheerful in spite of this knowledge. "I am grateful that fate has hit me so hard," she told me. "In my former life I was spoiled and did not take spiritual accomplishments seriously." Pointing through the window of the hut, she said, "This tree here is the only friend I have in my loneliness." Through that window she could see just one branch of a chestnut tree, and on the branch were two blossoms. "I often talk to this tree," she said to me. I was startled and didn't quite know how to take her words. Was she delirious? Did she have occasional hallucinations? Anxiously I asked her if the tree replied. "Yes." What did it say to her? She answered, "It said to me, 'I am here—I am here—I am life, eternal life.'"

We have stated that that which was ultimately responsible for the state of the prisoner's inner self was not so much the enumerated psychophysical causes as it was the result of a free decision. Psychological observations of the prisoners have shown that only the men who allowed their inner hold on their moral and spiritual selves to subside eventually fell victim to the camp's degenerating influences. The question now arises, what could, or should, have constituted this "inner hold"?

Former prisoners, when writing or relating their experiences, agree that the most depressing influence of all was that a prisoner could not know how long his term of imprisonment would be. He had been given no date for his release. (In our camp it was pointless even to talk about it.) Actually a prison term was not only uncertain but unlimited. A well-known research psychologist has pointed out that life in a concentration camp could be called a "provisional existence." We can add to this by defining it as a "provisional existence of unknown limit."

New arrivals usually knew nothing about the conditions at a camp. Those who had come back from other camps were obliged to keep silent, and from some camps no one had returned. On entering camp a change took place in the minds of the men. With the end of uncertainty there came the uncertainty of the end. It was impossible to foresee whether or when, if at all, this form of existence would end.

The Latin word *finis* has two meanings: the end or the finish, and a goal to reach. A man who could not see the end of his "provisional existence" was not able to aim at an ultimate goal in life. He ceased living for the future, in contrast to a man in normal life. Therefore the whole structure of his inner life changed; signs of decay set in which we know from other areas of life. The unemployed worker, for example, is in a similar position. His existence has become provisional and in a certain sense he cannot live for the future or aim at a goal. Research work done on unemployed miners has shown that they suffer from a peculiar sort of deformed time—inner time—which is a result of their unemployed state. Prisoners, too, suffered from this strange "time-experience." In camp, a small time unit, a day, for example, filled with hourly tortures and fatigue, appeared endless. A larger time unit, perhaps a week, seemed to pass very quickly. My comrades agreed when I said that in camp a day lasted longer than a week. How paradoxical was our time-experience! In this connection we are reminded of Thomas Mann's *The Magic Mountain*, which contains some very pointed psychological remarks. Mann studies the spiritual development of people who are in an analogous psychological position, i.e., tuberculosis patients in a sanatorium who also know no date for their release. They experience a similar existence—without a future and without a goal.

One of the prisoners, who on his arrival marched with a long column of new inmates from the station to the camp, told me later that he had felt as though he were marching at his own funeral. His life had seemed to him absolutely without future. He regarded it as over and done, as if he had already died. This feeling of lifelessness was intensified by other causes: in time, it was the limitlessness of the term of imprisonment which was most acutely felt; in space, the narrow limits of the prison. Anything outside the barbed wire became remote—out of reach and, in a way, unreal. The events and the people outside, all the normal life there, had a ghostly aspect for the prisoner. The outside life, that is, as much as he could see of it, appeared to him almost as it might have to a dead man who looked at it from another world.

A man who let himself decline because he could not see any future goal found himself occupied with retrospective thoughts. In a different connection, we have already spoken of the tendency there was to look into the past, to help make the present, with all its horrors, less real. But in robbing the present of its reality there lay a certain danger. It became easy to overlook the opportunities to make something positive of camp life, opportunities which really did exist. Regarding our "provisional existence" as unreal was in itself an important factor in causing the prisoners to lose their hold on life; everything in a way became pointless. Such people forgot that often it is just such an exceptionally difficult external situation which gives man the opportunity to grow spiritually beyond himself. Instead of taking the camp's difficulties as a test of their inner strength, they did not take their life seriously and despised it as something of no consequence. They preferred to close their eyes and to live in the past. Life for such people became meaningless.

Naturally only a few people were capable of reaching great spiritual heights. But a few were given the chance to attain human greatness even through their apparent worldly failure and death, an accomplishment which in ordinary circumstances they would never have achieved. To the others of us, the mediocre and the half-hearted, the words of Bismarck could be applied: "Life is like being at the dentist. You always think that the worst is still to come, and yet it is over already." Varying this, we could say that most men in a concentration camp believed that the real opportunities of life had passed. Yet, in reality, there was an opportunity and a challenge. One could make a victory of those experiences, turning life into an inner triumph, or one could ignore the challenge and simply vegetate, as did a majority of the prisoners.

Any attempt at fighting the camp's psychopathological influence on the prisoner by psychotherapeutic or psycho-hygienic methods had to aim at giving him inner strength by pointing out to him a future goal to which he could look forward. Instinctively some of the prisoners attempted to find one on their own. It is a peculiarity of man that he can only live by looking to the future—*sub specie aeternitatis*. And this is his salvation in the most difficult moments of his existence, although he sometimes has to force his mind to the task.

I remember a personal experience. Almost in tears from pain (I had terrible sores on my feet from wearing torn shoes), I limped a few kilometers with our long column of men from the camp to our work site. Very cold, bitter winds struck us. I kept thinking of the endless little problems of our miserable life. What would there be to eat tonight? If a piece of sausage came as extra ration, should I exchange it for a piece of bread? Should I trade my last cigarette, which was left from a bonus I received a fortnight ago, for a bowl of soup? How could I get a piece of wire to replace the fragment which served as one of my shoelaces? Would I get to our work site in time to join my usual working party or would I have to join another, which might have a brutal foreman? What could I do to get on good terms with the Capo, who could help me to obtain work in camp instead of undertaking this horribly long daily march?

I became disgusted with the state of affairs which compelled me, daily and hourly, to think of only such trivial things. I forced my thoughts to turn to another subject. Suddenly I saw myself standing on the platform of a well-lit, warm and pleasant lecture room. In front of me sat an attentive audience on comfortable upholstered seats. I was giving a lecture on the psychology of the concentration camp! All that oppressed me at that moment became objective, seen and described from the remote viewpoint of science. By this method I succeeded somehow in rising above the situation, above the sufferings of the moment, and I observed them as if they were already of the past. Both I and my troubles became the object of an interesting psychoscientific study undertaken by myself. What does Spinoza say in his *Ethics*? —*"Affectus, qui passio est, desinit esse passio simulatque eius claram et distinctam formamus ideam."* Emotion, which is suffering, ceases to be suffering as soon as we form a clear and precise picture of it.

The prisoner who had lost faith in the future—his future— was doomed. With his loss of belief in the future, he also lost his spiritual hold; he let himself decline and became subject to mental and physical decay. Usually this happened quite suddenly, in the form of a crisis, the symptoms of which were familiar to the experienced camp inmate. We all feared this moment—not for ourselves, which would have been point- less, but for our friends. Usually it began with the prisoner re- fusing one morning to get dressed and wash or to go out on the parade grounds. No entreaties, no blows, no threats had any effect. He just lay there, hardly moving. If this crisis was brought about by an illness, he refused to be taken to the sick- bay or to do anything to help himself. He simply gave up. There he remained, lying in his own excreta, and nothing bothered him any more.

I once had a dramatic demonstration of the close link be- tween the loss of faith in the future and this dangerous giving up. F——, my senior block warden, a fairly well-known com- poser and librettist, confided in me one day: "I would like to tell you something, Doctor. I have had a strange dream. A voice told me that I could wish for something, that I should only say what I wanted to know, and all my questions would be answered. What do you think I asked? That I would like to know when the war would be over for me. You know what I mean, Doctor—for me! I wanted to know when we, when our camp, would be liberated and our sufferings come to an end."

"And when did you have this dream?" I asked.

"In February, 1945," he answered. It was then the beginning of March.

"What did your dream voice answer?"

Furtively he whispered to me, "March thirtieth."

When F—— told me about his dream, he was still full of hope and convinced that the voice of his dream would be right. But as the promised day drew nearer, the war news which reached our camp made it appear very unlikely that we would be free on the promised date. On March twenty-ninth, F—— suddenly became ill and ran a high temperature. On March thirtieth, the day his prophecy had told him that the war and suffering would be over for him, he became delirious and lost consciousness. On March thirty-first, he was dead. To all outward appearances, he had died of typhus.

Those who know how close the connection is between the state of mind of a man—his courage and hope, or lack of them—and the state of immunity of his body will understand that the sudden loss of hope and courage can have a deadly effect. The ultimate cause of my friend's death was that the expected liberation did not come and he was severely disappointed. This suddenly lowered his body's resistance against the latent typhus infection. His faith in the future and his will to live had become paralyzed and his body fell victim to illness—and thus the voice of his dream was right after all.

The observations of this one case and the conclusion drawn from them are in accordance with something that was drawn to my attention by the chief doctor of our concentration camp. The death rate in the week between Christmas, 1944, and New Year's, 1945, increased in camp beyond all previous experience. In his opinion, the explanation for this increase did not lie in the harder working conditions or the deterioration of our food supplies or a change of weather or new epidemics. It was simply that the majority of the prisoners had lived in the naïve hope that they would be home again by Christmas. As the time drew near and there was no encouraging news, the prisoners lost courage and disappointment overcame them. This had a dangerous influence on their powers of resistance and a great number of them died.

As we said before, any attempt to restore a man's inner strength in the camp had first to succeed in showing him some future goal. Nietzsche's words, "He who has a *why* to live for can bear with almost any *how*," could be the guiding motto for all psychotherapeutic and psychohygienic efforts regarding prisoners. Whenever there was an opportunity for it, one had to give them a why—an aim—for their lives, in order to strengthen them to bear the terrible *how* of their existence. Woe to him who saw no more sense in his life, no aim, no purpose, and therefore no point in carrying on. He was soon lost. The typical reply with which such a man rejected all encouraging arguments was, "I have nothing to expect from life any more." What sort of answer can one give to that?

What was really needed was a fundamental change in our

attitude toward life. We had to learn ourselves and, further-more, we had to teach the despairing men, that *it did not re-ally matter what we expected from life, but rather what life expected from us.* We needed to stop asking about the mean-ing of life, and instead to think of ourselves as those who were being questioned by life—daily and hourly. Our answer must consist, not in talk and meditation, but in right action and in right conduct. Life ultimately means taking the responsibil-ity to find the right answer to its problems and to fulfill the tasks which it constantly sets for each individual.

These tasks, and therefore the meaning of life, differ from man to man, and from moment to moment. Thus it is impos-sible to define the meaning of life in a general way. Questions about the meaning of life can never be answered by sweep-ing statements. "Life" does not mean something vague, but something very real and concrete, just as life's tasks are also very real and concrete. They form man's destiny, which is dif-ferent and unique for each individual. No man and no destiny can be compared with any other man or any other destiny. No situation repeats itself, and each situation calls for a different response. Sometimes the situation in which a man finds him-self may require him to shape his own fate by action. At other times it is more advantageous for him to make use of an op-portunity for contemplation and to realize assets in this way. Sometimes man may be required simply to accept fate, to bear his cross. Every situation is distinguished by its unique-ness, and there is always only one right answer to the prob-lem posed by the situation at hand.

When a man finds that it is his destiny to suffer, he will

have to accept his suffering as his task; his single and unique task. He will have to acknowledge the fact that even in suffering he is unique and alone in the universe. No one can relieve him of his suffering or suffer in his place. His unique opportunity lies in the way in which he bears his burden.

For us, as prisoners, these thoughts were not speculations far removed from reality. They were the only thoughts that could be of help to us. They kept us from despair, even when there seemed to be no chance of coming out of it alive. Long ago we had passed the stage of asking what was the meaning of life, a naïve query which understands life as the attaining of some aim through the active creation of something of value. For us, the meaning of life embraced the wider cycles of life and death, of suffering and of dying.

Once the meaning of suffering had been revealed to us, we refused to minimize or alleviate the camp's tortures by ignoring them or harboring false illusions and entertaining artificial optimism. Suffering had become a task on which we did not want to turn our backs. We had realized its hidden opportunities for achievement, the opportunities which caused the poet Rilke to write, *"Wie viel ist aufzuleiden!"* (How much suffering there is to get through!). Rilke spoke of "getting through suffering" as others would talk of "getting through work." There was plenty of suffering for us to get through. Therefore, it was necessary to face up to the full amount of suffering, trying to keep moments of weakness and furtive tears to a minimum. But there was no need to be ashamed of tears, for tears bore witness that a man had the greatest of courage, the courage to suffer. Only very few realized that. Shamefacedly some confessed occasionally that they had wept, like the comrade who answered my question of how he had gotten over his edema, by confessing, "I have wept it out of my system."

The tender beginnings of a psychotherapy or psychohygiene were, when they were possible at all in the camp, either individual or collective in nature. The individual psychotherapeutic attempts were often a kind of "lifesaving procedure." These efforts were usually concerned with the prevention of suicides. A very strict camp ruling forbade any efforts to save a man who attempted suicide. It was forbidden, for example, to cut down a man who was trying to hang himself. Therefore, it was all important to prevent these attempts from occurring.

I remember two cases of would-be suicide, which bore a striking similarity to each other. Both men had talked of their intentions to commit suicide. Both used the typical argument —they had nothing more to expect from life. In both cases it was a question of getting them to realize that life was still expecting something from them; something in the future was expected of them. We found, in fact, that for the one it was his child whom he adored and who was waiting for him in a foreign country. For the other it was a thing, not a person. This man was a scientist and had written a series of books which still needed to be finished. His work could not be done by anyone else, any more than another person could ever take the place of the father in his child's affections.

This uniqueness and singleness which distinguishes each individual and gives a meaning to his existence has a bearing on creative work as much as it does on human love. When the impossibility of replacing a person is realized, it allows the responsibility which a man has for his existence and its continuance to appear in all its magnitude. A man who becomes conscious of the responsibility he bears toward a human being who affectionately waits for him, or to an unfinished work, will never be able to throw away his life. He knows the "why" for his existence, and will be able to bear almost any "how."

The opportunities for collective psychotherapy were naturally limited in camp. The right example was more effective than words could ever be. A senior block warden who did not side with the authorities had, by his just and encouraging behavior, a thousand opportunities to exert a far-reaching moral influence on those under his jurisdiction. The immediate influence of behavior is always more effective than that of words. But at times a word was effective too, when mental receptiveness had been intensified by some outer circumstances. I remember an incident when there was occasion for psychotherapeutic work on the inmates of a whole hut, due to an intensification of their receptiveness because of a certain external situation.

It had been a bad day. On parade, an announcement had been made about the many actions that would, from then on, be regarded as sabotage and therefore punishable by immediate death by hanging. Among these were crimes such as cutting small strips from our old blankets (in order to improvise ankle supports) and very minor "thefts." A few days previously a semi-starved prisoner had broken into the potato store to steal a few pounds of potatoes. The theft had been discovered and some prisoners had recognized the "burglar." When the camp authorities heard about it they ordered that the guilty man be given up to them or the whole camp would starve for a day. Naturally the 2,500 men preferred to fast.

On the evening of this day of fasting we lay in our earthen huts—in a very low mood. Very little was said and every word sounded irritable. Then, to make matters even worse, the light went out. Tempers reached their lowest ebb. But our senior block warden was a wise man. He improvised a little talk about all that was on our minds at that moment. He talked about the many comrades who had died in the last few days, either of sickness or of suicide. But he also mentioned what may have been the real reason for their deaths: giving up hope. He maintained that there should be some way of preventing possible future victims from reaching this extreme state. And it was to me that the warden pointed to give this advice.

God knows, I was not in the mood to give psychological explanations or to preach any sermons—to offer my comrades a kind of medical care of their souls. I was cold and hungry, irritable and tired, but I had to make the effort and use this unique opportunity. Encouragement was now more necessary than ever.

So I began by mentioning the most trivial of comforts first. I said that even in this Europe in the sixth winter of the Second World War, our situation was not the most terrible we could think of. I said that each of us had to ask himself what irreplaceable losses he had suffered up to then. I speculated that for most of them these losses had really been few. Whoever was still alive had reason for hope. Health, family, happiness, professional abilities, fortune, position in society —all these were things that could be achieved again or restored. After all, we still had all our bones intact. Whatever we had gone through could still be an asset to us in the future. And I quoted from Nietzsche: *"Was mich nicht umbringt, macht mich stärker."* (That which does not kill me, makes me stronger.)

Then I spoke about the future. I said that to the impartial the future must seem hopeless. I agreed that each of us could guess for himself how small were his chances of survival. I told them that although there was still no typhus epidemic in the camp, I estimated my own chances at about one in twenty. But I also told them that, in spite of this, I had no intention of losing hope and giving up. For no man knew what the future would bring, much less the next hour. Even if we could not expect any sensational military events in the next few days, who knew better than we, with our experience of camps, how great chances sometimes opened up, quite suddenly, at least for the individual. For instance, one might be attached unexpectedly to a special group with exceptionally good working conditions—for this was the kind of thing which constituted the "luck" of the prisoner.

But I did not only talk of the future and the veil which was drawn over it. I also mentioned the past; all its joys, and how its light shone even in the present darkness. Again I quoted a poet—to avoid sounding like a preacher myself—who had written, *"Was Du erlebst, kann keine Macht der Welt Dir rauben."* (What you have experienced, no power on earth can take from you.) Not only our experiences, but all we have done, whatever great thoughts we may have had, and all we have suffered, all this is not lost, though it is past; we have brought it into being. Having been is also a kind of being, and perhaps the surest kind.

Then I spoke of the many opportunities of giving life a

meaning. I told my comrades (who lay motionless, although occasionally a sigh could be heard) that human life, under any circumstances, never ceases to have a meaning, and that this infinite meaning of life includes suffering and dying, privation and death. I asked the poor creatures who listened to me attentively in the darkness of the hut to face up to the seriousness of our position. They must not lose hope but should keep their courage in the certainty that the hopelessness of our struggle did not detract from its dignity and its meaning. I said that someone looks down on each of us in difficult hours—a friend, a wife, somebody alive or dead, or a God— and he would not expect us to disappoint him. He would hope to find us suffering proudly—not miserably—knowing how to die.

And finally I spoke of our sacrifice, which had meaning in every case. It was in the nature of this sacrifice that it should appear to be pointless in the normal world, the world of material success. But in reality our sacrifice did have a meaning. Those of us who had any religious faith, I said frankly, could understand without difficulty. I told them of a comrade who on his arrival in camp had tried to make a pact with Heaven that his suffering and death should save the human being he loved from a painful end. For this man, suffering and death were meaningful; his was a sacrifice of the deepest significance. He did not want to die for nothing. None of us wanted that.

The purpose of my words was to find a full meaning in our life, then and there, in that hut and in that practically hopeless situation. I saw that my efforts had been successful. When the electric bulb flared up again, I saw the miserable figures of my friends limping toward me to thank me with tears in their eyes. But I have to confess here that only too rarely had I the inner strength to make contact with my companions in suffering and that I must have missed many opportunities for doing so.

We now come to the third stage of a prisoner's mental reactions: the psychology of the prisoner after his liberation. But prior to that we shall consider a question which the psychologist is asked frequently, especially when he has personal knowledge of these matters: What can you tell us about the psychological make-up of the camp guards? How is it possible that men of flesh and blood could treat others as so many prisoners say they have been treated? Having once heard these accounts and having come to believe that these things did happen, one is bound to ask how, psychologically, they could happen. To answer this question without going into great detail, a few things must be pointed out:

First, among the guards there were some sadists, sadists in the purest clinical sense.

Second, these sadists were always selected when a really severe detachment of guards was needed.

There was great joy at our work site when we had permission to warm ourselves for a few minutes (after two hours of work in the bitter frost) in front of a little stove which was fed with twigs and scraps of wood. But there were always some foremen who found a great pleasure in taking this comfort from us. How clearly their faces reflected this pleasure when they not only forbade us to stand there but turned over the stove and dumped its lovely fire into the snow! When the SS took a dislike to a person, there was always some special man in their ranks known to have a passion for, and to be highly specialized in, sadistic torture, to whom the unfortunate prisoner was sent.

Third, the feelings of the majority of the guards had been dulled by the number of years in which, in ever-increasing doses, they had witnessed the brutal methods of the camp. These morally and mentally hardened men at least refused to take active part in sadistic measures. But they did not prevent others from carrying them out.

Fourth, it must be stated that even among the guards there were some who took pity on us. I shall only mention the commander of the camp from which I was liberated. It was found after the liberation—only the camp doctor, a prisoner himself, had known of it previously—that this man had paid no small sum of money from his own pocket in order to purchase medicines for his prisoners from the nearest market town.[1] But the senior camp warden, a prisoner himself,

---

1. An interesting incident with reference to this SS commander is in regard to the attitude toward him of some of his Jewish prisoners. At the end of the war when the American troops liberated the prisoners from our camp, three young Hungarian Jews hid this commander in the Bavarian woods. Then they went to the commandant of the American Forces who was very eager to capture this SS commander and they said they would tell him where he was but only under certain conditions: the American commander must promise that absolutely no harm would come to this man. After a while, the American officer finally promised these young Jews that the SS commander when taken into captivity would be kept safe from harm. Not only did the American officer keep his promise but, as a matter of fact, the former SS commander of this concentration camp was in a sense restored to his command, for he supervised the collection of clothing among the nearby Bavarian villages, and its distribution to all of us who at that time still wore the clothes we had inherited from other inmates of Camp Auschwitz who were not as fortunate as we, having been sent to the gas chamber immediately upon their arrival at the railway station.

was harder than any of the SS guards. He beat the other prisoners at every slightest opportunity, while the camp commander, to my knowledge, never once lifted his hand against any of us.

It is apparent that the mere knowledge that a man was either a camp guard or a prisoner tells us almost nothing. Human kindness can be found in all groups, even those which as a whole it would be easy to condemn. The boundaries between groups overlapped and we must not try to simplify matters by saying that these men were angels and those were devils. Certainly, it was a considerable achievement for a guard or foreman to be kind to the prisoners in spite of all the camp's influences, and, on the other hand, the baseness of a prisoner who treated his own companions badly was exceptionally contemptible. Obviously the prisoners found the lack of character in such men especially upsetting, while they were profoundly moved by the smallest kindness received from any of the guards. I remember how one day a foreman secretly gave me a piece of bread which I knew he must have saved from his breakfast ration. It was far more than the small piece of bread which moved me to tears at that time. It was the human "something" which this man also gave to me—the word and look which accompanied the gift.

From all this we may learn that there are two races of men in this world, but only these two—the "race" of the decent man and the "race" of the indecent man. Both are found everywhere; they penetrate into all groups of society. No group consists entirely of decent or indecent people. In this sense, no group is of "pure race"—and therefore one occasionally found a decent fellow among the camp guards.

Life in a concentration camp tore open the human soul and exposed its depths. Is it surprising that in those depths we again found only human qualities which in their very nature were a mixture of good and evil? The rift dividing good from evil, which goes through all human beings, reaches into the lowest depths and becomes apparent even on the bottom of the abyss which is laid open by the concentration camp.

And now to the last chapter in the psychology of a concentration camp—the psychology of the prisoner who has been released. In describing the experiences of liberation, which naturally must be personal, we shall pick up the threads of that part of our narrative which told of the morning when the white flag was hoisted above the camp gates after days of high tension. This state of inner suspense was followed by total relaxation. But it would be quite wrong to think that we went mad with joy. What, then, did happen?

With tired steps we prisoners dragged ourselves to the camp gates. Timidly we looked around and glanced at each other questioningly. Then we ventured a few steps out of camp. This time no orders were shouted at us, nor was there any need to duck quickly to avoid a blow or kick. Oh no! This time the guards offered us cigarettes! We hardly recognized them at first; they had hurriedly changed into civilian clothes. We walked slowly along the road leading from the camp. Soon our legs hurt and threatened to buckle. But we limped on; we wanted to see the camp's surroundings for the first time with the eyes of free men. "Freedom"—we repeated to ourselves, and yet we could not grasp it. We had said this word so often during all the years we dreamed about it, that it had lost its meaning. Its reality did not penetrate into our consciousness; we could not grasp the fact that freedom was ours.

We came to meadows full of flowers. We saw and realized that they were there, but we had no feelings about them. The first spark of joy came when we saw a rooster with a tail of multicolored feathers. But it remained only a spark; we did not yet belong to this world.

In the evening when we all met again in our hut, one said secretly to the other, "Tell me, were you pleased today?"

And the other replied, feeling ashamed as he did not know that we all felt similarly, "Truthfully, no!" We had literally lost the ability to feel pleased and had to relearn it slowly.

Psychologically, what was happening to the liberated prisoners could be called "depersonalization." Everything appeared unreal, unlikely, as in a dream. We could not believe it was true. How often in the past years had we been deceived by dreams! We dreamt that the day of liberation had come, that we had been set free, had returned home, greeted our friends, embraced our wives, sat down at the table and started to tell of all the things we had gone through—even of how we had often seen the day of liberation in our dreams. And then— a whistle shrilled in our ears, the signal to get up, and our dreams of freedom came to an end. And now the dream had come true. But could we truly believe in it?

The body has fewer inhibitions than the mind. It made good use of the new freedom from the first moment on. It began to eat ravenously, for hours and days, even half the night. It is amazing what quantities one can eat. And when one of the prisoners was invited out by a friendly farmer in the neighborhood, he ate and ate and then drank coffee, which loosened his tongue, and he then began to talk, often for hours. The pressure which had been on his mind for years was released at last. Hearing him talk, one got the impression that he *had* to talk, that his desire to speak was irresistible. I have known people who have been under heavy pressure only for a short time (for example, through a cross-examination by the Gestapo) to have similar reactions. Many days passed, until not only the tongue was loosened, but something within oneself as well; then feeling suddenly broke through the strange fetters which had restrained it.

One day, a few days after the liberation, I walked through the country past flowering meadows, for miles and miles, toward the market town near the camp. Larks rose to the sky and I could hear their joyous song. There was no one to be seen for miles around; there was nothing but the wide earth and sky and the larks' jubilation and the freedom of space. I stopped, looked around, and up to the sky—and then I went down on my knees. At that moment there was very little I knew of myself or of the world—I had but one sentence in mind—always the same: "I called to the Lord from my narrow prison and He answered me in the freedom of space."

How long I knelt there and repeated this sentence memory can no longer recall. But I know that on that day, in that hour, my new life started. Step for step I progressed, until I again became a human being.

The way that led from the acute mental tension of the last days in camp (from that war of nerves to mental peace) was certainly not free from obstacles. It would be an error to think that a liberated prisoner was not in need of spiritual care any more. We have to consider that a man who has been under such enormous mental pressure for such a long time is naturally in some danger after his liberation, especially since the pressure was released quite suddenly. This danger (in the sense of psychological hygiene) is the psychological counterpart of the bends. Just as the physical health of the caisson worker would be endangered if he left his diver's chamber suddenly (where he is under enormous atmospheric pressure), so the man who has suddenly been liberated from mental pressure can suffer damage to his moral and spiritual health.

During this psychological phase one observed that people with natures of a more primitive kind could not escape the influences of the brutality which had surrounded them in camp life. Now, being free, they thought they could use their freedom licentiously and ruthlessly. The only thing that had changed for them was that they were now the oppressors instead of the oppressed. They became instigators, not objects, of willful force and injustice. They justified their behavior by their own terrible experiences. This was often revealed in apparently insignificant events. A friend was walking across a field with me toward the camp when suddenly we came to a field of green crops. Automatically, I avoided it, but he drew his arm through mine and dragged me through it. I stammered something about not treading down the young crops. He became annoyed, gave me an angry look and shouted, "You don't say! And hasn't enough been taken from us? My wife and child have been gassed—not to mention everything else—and you would forbid me to tread on a few stalks of oats!"

Only slowly could these men be guided back to the commonplace truth that no one has the right to do wrong, not even if wrong has been done to them. We had to strive to lead them back to this truth, or the consequences would have been much worse than the loss of a few thousand stalks of oats. I can still see the prisoner who rolled up his shirt sleeves, thrust his right hand under my nose and shouted, "May this hand be cut off if I don't stain it with blood on the day when I get home!" I want to emphasize that the man who said these words was not a bad fellow. He had been the best of comrades in camp and afterwards.

Apart from the moral deformity resulting from the sudden release of mental pressure, there were two other fundamental experiences which threatened to damage the character of the liberated prisoner: bitterness and disillusionment when he returned to his former life.

Bitterness was caused by a number of things he came up against in his former home town. When, on his return, a man found that in many places he was met only with a shrug of the shoulders and with hackneyed phrases, he tended to become bitter and to ask himself why he had gone through all that he had. When he heard the same phrases nearly everywhere— "We did not know about it," and "We, too, have suffered," then he asked himself, have they really nothing better to say to me?

The experience of disillusionment is different. Here it was not one's fellow man (whose superficiality and lack of feeling was so disgusting that one finally felt like creeping into a hole and neither hearing nor seeing human beings any more) but fate itself which seemed so cruel. A man who for years had thought he had reached the absolute limit of all possible suffering now found that suffering has no limits, and that he could suffer still more, and still more intensely.

When we spoke about attempts to give a man in camp mental courage, we said that he had to be shown something to look forward to in the future. He had to be reminded that life still waited for him, that a human being waited for his return. But after liberation? There were some men who found that no one awaited them. Woe to him who found that the person whose memory alone had given him courage in camp did not exist any more! Woe to him who, when the day of his dreams finally came, found it so different from all he had longed for! Perhaps he boarded a trolley, traveled out to the home which he had seen for years in his mind, and only in his mind, and pressed the bell, just as he has longed to do in thousands of dreams, only to find that the person who should open the door was not there, and would never be there again.

We all said to each other in camp that there could be no earthly happiness which could compensate for all we had suffered. We were not hoping for happiness—it was not that which gave us courage and gave meaning to our suffering, our sacrifices and our dying. And yet we were not prepared for unhappiness. This disillusionment, which awaited not a small number of prisoners, was an experience which these men have found very hard to get over and which, for a psychiatrist, is also very difficult to help them overcome. But this must not be a discouragement to him; on the contrary, it should provide an added stimulus.

But for every one of the liberated prisoners, the day comes when, looking back on his camp experiences, he can no longer understand how he endured it all. As the day of his lib-eration eventually came, when everything seemed to him like a beautiful dream, so also the day comes when all his camp experiences seem to him nothing but a nightmare.

The crowning experience of all, for the homecoming man, is the wonderful feeling that, after all he has suffered, there is nothing he need fear any more—except his God.

II

# LOGOTHERAPY
# IN A NUTSHELL

READERS OF MY SHORT AUTOBIOGRAPHICAL STORY usually ask for a fuller and more direct explanation of my therapeutic doctrine. Accordingly I added a brief section on logotherapy to the original edition of *From Death-Camp to Existentialism*. But that was not enough, and I have been besieged by requests for a more extended treatment. Therefore in the present edition I have completely rewritten and considerably expanded my account.

The assignment was not easy. To convey to the reader within a short space all the material which required twenty volumes in German is an almost hopeless task. I am reminded of the American doctor who once turned up in my office in Vienna and asked me, "Now, Doctor, are you a psychoanalyst?" Whereupon I replied, "Not exactly a psychoanalyst; let's say a psychotherapist." Then he continued questioning me: "What school do you stand for?" I answered, "It is my own theory; it is called *logotherapy*." "Can you tell me in one sentence what is meant by logotherapy?" he asked. "At least, what is the difference between psychoanalysis and lo-

---

This part, which has been revised and updated, first appeared as "Basic Concepts of Logotherapy" in the 1962 edition of *Man's Search for Meaning*.

gotherapy?" "Yes," I said, "but in the first place, can you tell me in one sentence what you think the essence of psychoanalysis is?" This was his answer: "During psychoanalysis, the patient must lie down on a couch and tell you things which sometimes are very disagreeable to tell." Whereupon I immediately retorted with the following improvisation: "Now, in logotherapy the patient may remain sitting erect but he must hear things which sometimes are very disagreeable to hear."

Of course, this was meant facetiously and not as a capsule version of logotherapy. However, there is something in it, inasmuch as logotherapy, in comparison with psychoanalysis, is a method less *retrospective* and less *introspective*. Logotherapy focuses rather on the future, that is to say, on the meanings to be fulfilled by the patient in his future. (Logotherapy, indeed, is a meaning-centered psychotherapy.) At the same time, logotherapy defocuses all the vicious-circle formations and feedback mechanisms which play such a great role in the development of neuroses. Thus, the typical self-centeredness of the neurotic is broken up instead of being continually fostered and reinforced.

To be sure, this kind of statement is an oversimplification; yet in logotherapy the patient is actually confronted with and reoriented toward the meaning of his life. And to make him aware of this meaning can contribute much to his ability to overcome his neurosis.

Let me explain why I have employed the term "logotherapy" as the name for my theory. *Logos* is a Greek word which denotes "meaning." Logotherapy, or, as it has been called by some authors, "The Third Viennese School of Psychotherapy," focuses on the meaning of human existence as well as on man's search for such a meaning. According to logotherapy, this striving to find a meaning in one's life is the primary motivational force in man. That is why I speak of a *will to meaning* in contrast to the pleasure principle (or, as we could also term it, the *will to pleasure*) on which Freudian psychoanalysis is centered, as well as in contrast to the *will to power* on which Adlerian psychology, using the term "striving for superiority," is focused.

## The Will to Meaning

Man's search for meaning is the primary motivation in his life and not a "secondary rationalization" of instinctual drives. This meaning is unique and specific in that it must and can be fulfilled by him alone; only then does it achieve a significance which will satisfy his own *will* to meaning. There are some authors who contend that meanings and values are "nothing but defense mechanisms, reaction formations and sublimations." But as for myself, I would not be willing to live merely for the sake of my "defense mechanisms," nor would I be ready to die merely for the sake of my "reaction formations." Man, however, is able to live and even to die for the sake of his ideals and values!

A public-opinion poll was conducted a few years ago in France. The results showed that 89 percent of the people polled admitted that man needs "something" for the sake of which to live. Moreover, 61 percent conceded that there was something, or someone, in their own lives for whose sake they were even ready to die. I repeated this poll at my hospital department in Vienna among both the patients and the personnel, and the outcome was practically the same as among the thousands of people screened in France; the difference was only 2 percent.

Another statistical survey, of 7,948 students at forty-eight colleges, was conducted by social scientists from Johns Hopkins University. Their preliminary report is part of a two-year study sponsored by the National Institute of Mental Health. Asked what they considered "very important" to them now, 16 percent of the students checked "making a lot of money"; 78 percent said their first goal was "finding a purpose and meaning to my life."

Of course, there may be some cases in which an individual's concern with values is really a camouflage of hidden inner conflicts; but, if so, they represent the exceptions from the rule rather than the rule itself. In these cases we have actually to deal with pseudovalues, and as such they have to be unmasked. Unmasking, however, should stop as soon as one is confronted with what is authentic and genuine in man, e.g., man's desire for a life that is as meaningful as possible. If it does not stop then, the only thing that the "unmasking psychologist" really unmasks is his own "hidden motive"— namely, his unconscious need to debase and depreciate what is genuine, what is genuinely human, in man.

### Existential Frustration

Man's will to meaning can also be frustrated, in which case logotherapy speaks of "existential frustration." The term "existential" may be used in three ways: to refer to (1) *existence* itself, i.e., the specifically human mode of being; (2) the *mean-*

*ing* of existence; and (3) the striving to find a concrete meaning in personal existence, that is to say, the *will* to meaning.

Existential frustration can also result in neuroses. For this type of neuroses, logotherapy has coined the term "noögenic neuroses" in contrast to neuroses in the traditional sense of the word, i.e., psychogenic neuroses. Noögenic neuroses have their origin not in the psychological but rather in the "noölogical" (from the Greek *noös* meaning mind) dimension of human existence. This is another logotherapeutic term which denotes anything pertaining to the specifically human dimension.

### Noögenic Neuroses

Noögenic neuroses do not emerge from conflicts between drives and instincts but rather from existential problems. Among such problems, the frustration of the will to meaning plays a large role.

It is obvious that in noögenic cases the appropriate and adequate therapy is not psychotherapy in general but rather logotherapy; a therapy, that is, which dares to enter the specifically human dimension.

Let me quote the following instance: A high-ranking American diplomat came to my office in Vienna in order to continue psychoanalytic treatment which he had begun five years previously with an analyst in New York. At the outset I asked him why he thought he should be analyzed, why his analysis had been started in the first place. It turned out that the patient was discontented with his career and found it most difficult to comply with American foreign policy. His analyst, however, had told him again and again that he should try to reconcile himself with his father; because the government of the U.S. as well as his superiors were "nothing but" father images and, consequently, his dissatisfaction with his job was due to the hatred he unconsciously harbored toward his father. Through an analysis lasting five years, the patient had been prompted more and more to accept his analyst's interpretations until he finally was unable to see the forest of reality for the trees of symbols and images. After a few interviews, it was clear that his will to meaning was frustrated by his vocation, and he actually longed to be engaged in some other kind of work. As there was no reason for not giving up his profession and embarking on a different one, he did so, with most gratifying results. He has remained contented in this new occupation for over five years, as he recently reported. I doubt that, in this case, I was dealing with a neurotic condition at all, and that is why I thought that he did not need any psychotherapy, nor even logotherapy, for the simple reason that he was not actually a patient. Not every conflict is necessarily neurotic; some amount of conflict is normal and healthy. In a similar sense suffering is not always a pathological phenomenon; rather than being a symptom of neurosis, suffering may well be a human achievement, especially if the suffering grows out of existential frustration. I would strictly deny that one's search for a meaning to his existence, or even his doubt of it, in every case is derived from, or results in, any disease. Existential frustration is in itself neither pathological nor pathogenic. A man's concern, even his despair, over the worthwhileness of life is an *existential distress* but by no means a *mental disease*. It may well be that interpreting the first in terms of the latter motivates a doctor to bury his patient's existential despair under a heap of tranquilizing drugs. It is his task, rather, to pilot the patient through his existential crises of growth and development.

Logotherapy regards its assignment as that of assisting the patient to find meaning in his life. Inasmuch as logotherapy makes him aware of the hidden *logos* of his existence, it is an analytical process. To this extent, logotherapy resembles psychoanalysis. However, in logotherapy's attempt to make something conscious again it does not restrict its activity to *instinctual* facts within the individual's unconscious but also cares for *existential* realities, such as the potential meaning of his existence to be fulfilled as well as his *will* to meaning. Any analysis, however, even when it refrains from including the noölogical dimension in its therapeutic process, tries to make the patient aware of what he actually longs for in the depth of his being. Logotherapy deviates from psychoanalysis insofar as it considers man a being whose main concern consists in fulfilling a meaning, rather than in the mere gratification and satisfaction of drives and instincts, or in merely reconciling the conflicting claims of id, ego and superego, or in the mere adaptation and adjustment to society and environment.

## Noö-Dynamics

To be sure, man's search for meaning may arouse inner tension rather than inner equilibrium. However, precisely such tension is an indispensable prerequisite of mental health. There is nothing in the world, I venture to say, that would so effectively help one to survive even the worst conditions as the knowledge that there is a meaning in one's life. There is much wisdom in the words of Nietzsche: "He who has a *why* to live for can bear almost any *how*." I can see in these words a motto which holds true for any psychotherapy. In the Nazi concentration camps, one could have witnessed that those who knew that there was a task waiting for them to fulfill were most apt to survive. The same conclusion has since been reached by other authors of books on concentration camps, and also by psychiatric investigations into Japanese, North Korean and North Vietnamese prisoner-of-war camps.

As for myself, when I was taken to the concentration camp of Auschwitz, a manuscript of mine ready for publication was confiscated.[1] Certainly, my deep desire to write this manuscript anew helped me to survive the rigors of the camps I was in. For instance, when in a camp in Bavaria I fell ill with typhus fever, I jotted down on little scraps of paper many notes intended to enable me to rewrite the manuscript, should I live to the day of liberation. I am sure that this reconstruction of my lost manuscript in the dark barracks of a Bavarian concentration camp assisted me in overcoming the danger of cardiovascular collapse.

Thus it can be seen that mental health is based on a certain degree of tension, the tension between what one has already achieved and what one still ought to accomplish, or the

---

1. It was the first version of my first book, the English translation of which was published by Alfred A. Knopf, New York, in 1955, under the title *The Doctor and the Soul: An Introduction to Logotherapy.*

gap between what one is and what one should become. Such a tension is inherent in the human being and therefore is indispensable to mental well-being. We should not, then, be hesitant about challenging man with a potential meaning for him to fulfill. It is only thus that we evoke his will to meaning from its state of latency. I consider it a dangerous misconception of mental hygiene to assume that what man needs in the first place is equilibrium or, as it is called in biology, "homeostasis," i.e., a tensionless state. What man actually needs is not a tensionless state but rather the striving and struggling for a worthwhile goal, a freely chosen task. What he needs is not the discharge of tension at any cost but the call of a potential meaning waiting to be fulfilled by him. What man needs is not homeostasis but what I call "noö-dynamics," i.e., the existential dynamics in a polar field of tension where one pole is represented by a meaning that is to be fulfilled and the other pole by the man who has to fulfill it. And one should not think that this holds true only for normal conditions; in neurotic individuals, it is even more valid. If architects want to strengthen a decrepit arch, they *increase* the load which is laid upon it, for thereby the parts are joined more firmly together. So if therapists wish to foster their patients' mental health, they should not be afraid to create a sound amount of tension through a reorientation toward the meaning of one's life.

Having shown the beneficial impact of meaning orientation, I turn to the detrimental influence of that feeling of which so many patients complain today, namely, the feeling of the total and ultimate meaninglessness of their lives. They lack the awareness of a meaning worth living for. They are haunted by the experience of their inner emptiness, a void within themselves; they are caught in that situation which I have called the "existential vacuum."

## The Existential Vacuum

The existential vacuum is a widespread phenomenon of the twentieth century. This is understandable; it may be due to a twofold loss which man has had to undergo since he became a truly human being. At the beginning of human history, man lost some of the basic animal instincts in which an animal's behavior is imbedded and by which it is secured. Such security, like Paradise, is closed to man forever; man has to make choices. In addition to this, however, man has suffered another loss in his more recent development inasmuch as the traditions which buttressed his behavior are now rapidly diminishing. No instinct tells him what he has to do, and no tradition tells him what he ought to do; sometimes he does not even know what he wishes to do. Instead, he either wishes to do what other people do (conformism) or he does what other people wish him to do (totalitarianism).

A statistical survey recently revealed that among my European students, 25 percent showed a more-or-less marked degree of existential vacuum. Among my American students it was not 25 but 60 percent.

The existential vacuum manifests itself mainly in a state of boredom. Now we can understand Schopenhauer when he said that mankind was apparently doomed to vacillate eternally between the two extremes of distress and boredom. In actual fact, boredom is now causing, and certainly bringing to psychiatrists, more problems to solve than distress. And these problems are growing increasingly crucial, for progressive automation will probably lead to an enormous increase in the leisure hours available to the average worker. The pity of it is that many of these will not know what to do with all their newly acquired free time.

Let us consider, for instance, "Sunday neurosis," that kind of depression which afflicts people who become aware of the lack of content in their lives when the rush of the busy week is over and the void within themselves becomes manifest. Not a few cases of suicide can be traced back to this existential vacuum. Such widespread phenomena as depression, aggression and addiction are not understandable unless we recognize the existential vacuum underlying them. This is also true of the crises of pensioners and aging people.

Moreover, there are various masks and guises under which the existential vacuum appears. Sometimes the frustrated will to meaning is vicariously compensated for by a will to power, including the most primitive form of the will to power, the will to money. In other cases, the place of frustrated will to meaning is taken by the will to pleasure. That is why existential frustration often eventuates in sexual compensation. We can observe in such cases that the sexual libido becomes rampant in the existential vacuum.

An analogous event occurs in neurotic cases. There are certain types of feedback mechanisms and vicious-circle formations which I will touch upon later. One can observe again and again, however, that this symptomatology has invaded an existential vacuum wherein it then continues to flourish.

In such patients, what we have to deal with is not a noögenic neurosis. However, we will never succeed in having the patient overcome his condition if we have not supplemented the psychotherapeutic treatment with logotherapy. For by filling the existential vacuum, the patient will be prevented from suffering further relapses. Therefore, logotherapy is indicated not only in noögenic cases, as pointed out above, but also in psychogenic cases, and sometimes even the somatogenic (pseudo-) neuroses. Viewed in this light, a statement once made by Magda B. Arnold is justified: "Every therapy must in some way, no matter how restricted, also be logotherapy."[2]

Let us now consider what we can do if a patient asks what the meaning of his life *is*.

## The Meaning of Life

I doubt whether a doctor can answer this question in general terms. For the meaning of life differs from man to man, from day to day and from hour to hour. What matters, therefore, is not the meaning of life in general but rather the specific meaning of a person's life at a given moment. To put the question in general terms would be comparable to the question posed to a chess champion: "Tell me, Master, what is the best move in the world?" There simply is no such thing as the best or even a good move apart from a particular situation in a game and the particular personality of one's opponent. The same holds for human existence. One should not search for

---

2. Magda B. Arnold and John A. Gasson, *The Human Person*, Ronald Press, New York, 1954, p. 618.

an abstract meaning of life. Everyone has his own specific vocation or mission in life to carry out a concrete assignment which demands fulfillment. Therein he cannot be replaced, nor can his life be repeated. Thus, everyone's task is as unique as is his specific opportunity to implement it.

As each situation in life represents a challenge to man and presents a problem for him to solve, the question of the meaning of life may actually be reversed. Ultimately, man should not ask what the meaning of his life is, but rather he must recognize that it is *he* who is asked. In a word, each man is questioned by life; and he can only answer to life by *answering for* his own life; to life he can only respond by being responsible. Thus, logotherapy sees in responsibleness the very essence of human existence.

## The Essence of Existence

This emphasis on responsibleness is reflected in the categorical imperative of logotherapy, which is: "Live as if you were living already for the second time and as if you had acted the first time as wrongly as you are about to act now!" It seems to me that there is nothing which would stimulate a man's sense of responsibleness more than this maxim, which invites him to imagine first that the present is past and, second, that the past may yet be changed and amended. Such a precept confronts him with life's *finiteness* as well as the *finality* of what he makes out of both his life and himself.

Logotherapy tries to make the patient fully aware of his own responsibleness; therefore, it must leave to him the option for what, to what, or to whom he understands himself to be responsible. That is why a logotherapist is the least tempted of all psychotherapists to impose value judgments on his patients, for he will never permit the patient to pass to the doctor the responsibility of judging.

It is, therefore, up to the patient to decide whether he should interpret his life task as being responsible to society or to his own conscience. There are people, however, who do not interpret their own lives merely in terms of a task assigned to them but also in terms of the taskmaster who has assigned it to them.

Logotherapy is neither teaching nor preaching. It is as far removed from logical reasoning as it is from moral exhortation. To put it figuratively, the role played by a logotherapist is that of an eye specialist rather than that of a painter. A painter tries to convey to us a picture of the world as he sees it; an ophthalmologist tries to enable us to see the world as it really is. The logotherapist's role consists of widening and broadening the visual field of the patient so that the whole spectrum of potential meaning becomes conscious and visible to him.

By declaring that man is responsible and must actualize the potential meaning of his life, I wish to stress that the true meaning of life is to be discovered in the world rather than within man or his own psyche, as though it were a closed system. I have termed this constitutive characteristic "the self-transcendence of human existence." It denotes the fact that being human always points, and is directed, to something, or someone, other than oneself—be it a meaning to fulfill or another human being to encounter. The more one forgets himself—by giving himself to a cause to serve or another per-

son to love—the more human he is and the more he actu-
alizes himself. What is called self-actualization is not an at-
tainable aim at all, for the simple reason that the more one
would strive for it, the more he would miss it. In other words,
self-actualization is possible only as a side-effect of self-
transcendence.

Thus far we have shown that the meaning of life always
changes, but that it never ceases to be. According to logotherapy, we can discover this meaning in life in three different ways: (1) by creating a work or doing a deed; (2) by
experiencing something or encountering someone; and (3)
by the attitude we take toward unavoidable suffering. The
first, the way of achievement or accomplishment, is quite obvious. The second and third need further elaboration.

The second way of finding a meaning in life is by experiencing something—such as goodness, truth and beauty—by
experiencing nature and culture or, last but not least, by experiencing another human being in his very uniqueness—by
loving him.

### The Meaning of Love

Love is the only way to grasp another human being in the
innermost core of his personality. No one can become fully
aware of the very essence of another human being unless he
loves him. By his love he is enabled to see the essential traits
and features in the beloved person; and even more, he sees
that which is potential in him, which is not yet actualized
but yet ought to be actualized. Furthermore, by his love, the
loving person enables the beloved person to actualize these

potentialities. By making him aware of what he can be and of what he should become, he makes these potentialities come true.

In logotherapy, love is not interpreted as a mere epiphenomenon[3] of sexual drives and instincts in the sense of a so-called sublimation. Love is as primary a phenomenon as sex. Normally, sex is a mode of expression for love. Sex is justified, even sanctified, as soon as, but only as long as, it is a vehicle of love. Thus love is not understood as a mere side-effect of sex; rather, sex is a way of expressing the experience of that ultimate togetherness which is called love.

The third way of finding a meaning in life is by suffering.

## The Meaning of Suffering

We must never forget that we may also find meaning in life even when confronted with a hopeless situation, when facing a fate that cannot be changed. For what then matters is to bear witness to the uniquely human potential at its best, which is to transform a personal tragedy into a triumph, to turn one's predicament into a human achievement. When we are no longer able to change a situation—just think of an incurable disease such as inoperable cancer—we are challenged to change ourselves.

Let me cite a clear-cut example: Once, an elderly general practitioner consulted me because of his severe depression. He could not overcome the loss of his wife who had died two years before and whom he had loved above all else. Now, how

---

3. A phenomenon that occurs as the result of a primary phenomenon.

could I help him? What should I tell him? Well, I refrained from telling him anything but instead confronted him with the question, "What would have happened, Doctor, if you had died first, and your wife would have had to survive you?" "Oh," he said, "for her this would have been terrible; how she would have suffered!" Whereupon I replied, "You see, Doctor, such a suffering has been spared her, and it was you who have spared her this suffering—to be sure, at the price that now you have to survive and mourn her." He said no word but shook my hand and calmly left my office. In some way, suffering ceases to be suffering at the moment it finds a meaning, such as the meaning of a sacrifice.

Of course, this was no therapy in the proper sense since, first, his despair was no disease; and second, I could not change his fate; I could not revive his wife. But in that moment I did succeed in changing his *attitude* toward his unalterable fate inasmuch as from that time on he could at least see a meaning in his suffering. It is one of the basic tenets of logotherapy that man's main concern is not to gain pleasure or to avoid pain but rather to see a meaning in his life. That is why man is even ready to suffer, on the condition, to be sure, that his suffering has a meaning.

But let me make it perfectly clear that in no way is suffering *necessary* to find meaning. I only insist that meaning is possible even in spite of suffering—provided, certainly, that the suffering is unavoidable. If it *were* avoidable, however, the meaningful thing to do would be to remove its cause, be it psychological, biological or political. To suffer unnecessarily is masochistic rather than heroic.

Edith Weisskopf-Joelson, before her death professor of

psychology at the University of Georgia, contended, in her article on logotherapy, that "our current mental-hygiene philosophy stresses the idea that people ought to be happy, that unhappiness is a symptom of maladjustment. Such a value system might be responsible for the fact that the burden of unavoidable unhappiness is increased by unhappiness about being unhappy."[4] And in another paper she expressed the hope that logotherapy "may help counteract certain unhealthy trends in the present-day culture of the United States, where the incurable sufferer is given very little opportunity to be proud of his suffering and to consider it ennobling rather than degrading" so that "he is not only unhappy, but also ashamed of being unhappy."[5]

There are situations in which one is cut off from the opportunity to do one's work or to enjoy one's life; but what never can be ruled out is the unavoidability of suffering. In accepting this challenge to suffer bravely, life has a meaning up to the last moment, and it retains this meaning literally to the end. In other words, life's meaning is an unconditional one, for it even includes the potential meaning of unavoidable suffering.

Let me recall that which was perhaps the deepest experience I had in the concentration camp. The odds of surviving the camp were no more than one in twenty-eight, as can easily be verified by exact statistics. It did not even seem possible, let alone probable, that the manuscript of my first book,

---

4. "Some Comments on a Viennese School of Psychiatry," *The Journal of Abnormal and Social Psychology*, 51 (1955), pp. 701–3.

5. "Logotherapy and Existential Analysis," *Acta Psychotherapeutica*, 6 (1958), pp. 193–204.

which I had hidden in my coat when I arrived at Auschwitz, would ever be rescued. Thus, I had to undergo and to overcome the loss of my mental child. And now it seemed as if nothing and no one would survive me; neither a physical nor a mental child of my own! So I found myself confronted with the question whether under such circumstances my life was ultimately void of any meaning.

Not yet did I notice that an answer to this question with which I was wrestling so passionately was already in store for me, and that soon thereafter this answer would be given to me. This was the case when I had to surrender my clothes and in turn inherited the worn-out rags of an inmate who had already been sent to the gas chamber immediately after his arrival at the Auschwitz railway station. Instead of the many pages of my manuscript, I found in a pocket of the newly acquired coat one single page torn out of a Hebrew prayer book, containing the most important Jewish prayer, *Shema Yisrael*. How should I have interpreted such a "coincidence" other than as a challenge to *live* my thoughts instead of merely putting them on paper?

A bit later, I remember, it seemed to me that I would die in the near future. In this critical situation, however, my concern was different from that of most of my comrades. Their question was, "Will we survive the camp? For, if not, all this suffering has no meaning." The question which beset me was, "Has all this suffering, this dying around us, a meaning? For, if not, then ultimately there is no meaning to survival; for a life whose meaning depends upon such a happenstance—as whether one escapes or not—ultimately would not be worth living at all."

### Meta-Clinical Problems

More and more, a psychiatrist is approached today by patients who confront him with human problems rather than neurotic symptoms. Some of the people who nowadays call on a psychiatrist would have seen a pastor, priest or rabbi in former days. Now they often refuse to be handed over to a clergyman and instead confront the doctor with questions such as, "What is the meaning of my life?"

### A Logodrama

I should like to cite the following instance: Once, the mother of a boy who had died at the age of eleven years was admitted to my hospital department after a suicide attempt. Dr. Kurt Kocourek invited her to join a therapeutic group, and it happened that I stepped into the room where he was conducting a psychodrama. She was telling her story. At the death of her boy she was left alone with another, older son, who was crippled, suffering from the effects of infantile paralysis. The poor boy had to be moved around in a wheelchair. His mother, however, rebelled against her fate. But when she tried to commit suicide together with him, it was the crippled son who prevented her from doing so; he liked living! For him, life had remained meaningful. Why was it not so for his mother? How could her life still have a meaning? And how could we help her to become aware of it?

Improvising, I participated in the discussion, and questioned another woman in the group. I asked her how old she was and she answered, "Thirty." I replied, "No, you are not thirty but instead eighty and lying on your deathbed. And now you are looking back on your life, a life which was childless but full of financial success and social prestige." And then I invited her to imagine what she would feel in this situation. "What will you think of it? What will you say to yourself?" Let me quote what she actually said from a tape which was recorded during that session. "Oh, I married a millionaire, I had an easy life full of wealth, and I lived it up! I flirted with men; I teased them! But now I am eighty; I have no children of my own. Looking back as an old woman, I cannot see what all that was for; actually, I must say, my life was a failure!"

I then invited the mother of the handicapped son to imagine herself similarly looking back over *her* life. Let us listen to what she had to say as recorded on the tape: "I wished to have children and this wish has been granted to me; one boy died; the other, however, the crippled one, would have been sent to an institution if I had not taken over his care. Though he is crippled and helpless, he is after all my boy. And so I have made a fuller life possible for him; I have made a better human being out of my son." At this moment, there was an outburst of tears and, crying, she continued: "As for myself, I can look back peacefully on my life; for I can say my life was full of meaning, and I have tried hard to fulfill it; I have done my best—I have done the best for my son. My life was no failure!" Viewing her life as if from her deathbed, she had suddenly been able to see a meaning in it, a meaning which even included all of her sufferings. By the same token, however, it had become clear as well that a life of short duration, like that, for example, of her dead boy, could be so rich in joy and love that it could contain more meaning than a life lasting eighty years.

After a while I proceeded to another question, this time addressing myself to the whole group. The question was whether an ape which was being used to develop poliomyelitis serum, and for this reason punctured again and again, would ever be able to grasp the meaning of its suffering. Unanimously, the group replied that of course it would not; with its limited intelligence, it could not enter into the world of man, i.e., the only world in which the meaning of its suffering would be understandable. Then I pushed forward with the following question: "And what about man? Are you sure that the human world is a terminal point in the evolution of the cosmos? Is it not conceivable that there is still another dimension, a world beyond man's world; a world in which the question of an ultimate meaning of human suffering would find an answer?"

### The Super-Meaning

This ultimate meaning necessarily exceeds and surpasses the finite intellectual capacities of man; in logotherapy, we speak in this context of a super-meaning. What is demanded of man is not, as some existential philosophers teach, to endure the meaninglessness of life, but rather to bear his incapacity to grasp its unconditional meaningfulness in rational terms. *Logos* is deeper than logic.

A psychiatrist who goes beyond the concept of the super-meaning will sooner or later be embarrassed by his patients, just as I was when my daughter at about six years of age asked me the question, "Why do we speak of the *good* Lord?" Whereupon I said, "Some weeks ago, you were suffering from measles, and then the *good* Lord sent you full recovery." However, the little girl was not content; she retorted, "Well, but please, Daddy, do not forget: in the first place, he had sent me the measles."

However, when a patient stands on the firm ground of religious belief, there can be no objection to making use of the therapeutic effect of his religious convictions and thereby drawing upon his spiritual resources. In order to do so, the psychiatrist may put himself in the place of the patient. That is exactly what I did once, for instance, when a rabbi from Eastern Europe turned to me and told me his story. He had lost his first wife and their six children in the concentration camp of Auschwitz where they were gassed, and now it turned out that his second wife was sterile. I observed that procreation is not the only meaning of life, for then life in itself would become meaningless, and something which in itself is meaningless cannot be rendered meaningful merely by its perpetuation. However, the rabbi evaluated his plight as an orthodox Jew in terms of despair that there was no son of his own who would ever say Kaddish[6] for him after his death.

But I would not give up. I made a last attempt to help him by inquiring whether he did not hope to see his children again in Heaven. However, my question was followed by an outburst of tears, and now the true reason for his despair came to the fore: he explained that his children, since they died

_____

6. A prayer for the dead.

as innocent martyrs,[7] were thus found worthy of the highest place in Heaven, but as for himself he could not expect, as an old, sinful man, to be assigned the same place. I did not give up but retorted, "Is it not conceivable, Rabbi, that precisely this was the meaning of your surviving your children: that you may be purified through these years of suffering, so that finally you, too, though not innocent like your children, may *become* worthy of joining them in Heaven? Is it not written in the Psalms that God preserves all your tears?[8] So perhaps none of your sufferings were in vain." For the first time in many years he found relief from his suffering through the new point of view which I was able to open up to him.

### Life's Transitoriness

Those things which seem to take meaning away from human life include not only suffering but dying as well. I never tire of saying that the only really transitory aspects of life are the potentialities; but as soon as they are actualized, they are rendered realities at that very moment; they are saved and delivered into the past, wherein they are rescued and preserved from transitoriness. For, in the past, nothing is irretrievably lost but everything irrevocably stored.

Thus, the transitoriness of our existence in no way makes it meaningless. But it does constitute our responsibleness; for everything hinges upon our realizing the essentially tran-

---

7. *L'kiddush hasbem*, i.e., for the sanctification of God's name.

8. "Thou hast kept count of my tossings; put thou my tears in thy bottle! Are they not in thy book?" (Ps. 56, 8.)

sitory possibilities. Man constantly makes his choice concerning the mass of present potentialities; which of these will be condemned to nonbeing and which will be actualized? Which choice will be made an actuality once and forever, an immortal "footprint in the sands of time"? At any moment, man must decide, for better or for worse, what will be the monument of his existence.

Usually, to be sure, man considers only the stubble field of transitoriness and overlooks the full granaries of the past, wherein he had salvaged once and for all his deeds, his joys and also his sufferings. Nothing can be undone, and nothing can be done away with. I should say *having been* is the surest kind of being.

Logotherapy, keeping in mind the essential transitoriness of human existence, is not pessimistic but rather activistic. To express this point figuratively we might say: The pessimist resembles a man who observes with fear and sadness that his wall calendar, from which he daily tears a sheet, grows thinner with each passing day. On the other hand, the person who attacks the problems of life actively is like a man who removes each successive leaf from his calendar and files it neatly and carefully away with its predecessors, after first having jotted down a few diary notes on the back. He can reflect with pride and joy on all the richness set down in these notes, on all the life he has already lived to the fullest. What will it matter to him if he notices that he is growing old? Has he any reason to envy the young people whom he sees, or wax nostalgic over his own lost youth? What reasons has he to envy a young person? For the possibilities that a young person has, the future which is in store for him? "No, thank you," he will think.

"Instead of possibilities, I have realities in my past, not only the reality of work done and of love loved, but of sufferings bravely suffered. These sufferings are even the things of which I am most proud, though these are things which cannot inspire envy."

### Logotherapy as a Technique

A realistic fear, like the fear of death, cannot be tranquilized away by its psychodynamic interpretation; on the other hand, a neurotic fear, such as agoraphobia, cannot be cured by philosophical understanding. However, logotherapy has developed a special technique to handle such cases, too. To understand what is going on whenever this technique is used, we take as a starting point a condition which is frequently observed in neurotic individuals, namely, anticipatory anxiety. It is characteristic of this fear that it produces precisely that of which the patient is afraid. An individual, for example, who is afraid of blushing when he enters a large room and faces many people will actually be more prone to blush under these circumstances. In this context, one might amend the saying "The wish is father to the thought" to "The fear is mother of the event."

Ironically enough, in the same way that fear brings to pass what one is afraid of, likewise a forced intention makes impossible what one forcibly wishes. This excessive intention, or "hyper-intention," as I call it, can be observed particularly in cases of sexual neurosis. The more a man tries to demonstrate his sexual potency or a woman her ability to experience orgasm, the less they are able to succeed. Pleasure is, and must remain, a side-effect or by-product, and is destroyed and spoiled to the degree to which it is made a goal in itself.

In addition to excessive intention as described above, excessive attention, or "hyper-reflection," as it is called in logotherapy, may also be pathogenic (that is, lead to sickness). The following clinical report will indicate what I mean: A young woman came to me complaining of being frigid. The case history showed that in her childhood she had been sexually abused by her father. However, it had not been this traumatic experience in itself which had eventuated in her sexual neurosis, as could easily be evidenced. For it turned out that, through reading popular psychoanalytic literature, the patient had lived constantly with the fearful expectation of the toll which her traumatic experience would someday take. This anticipatory anxiety resulted both in excessive intention to confirm her femininity and excessive attention centered upon herself rather than upon her partner. This was enough to incapacitate the patient for the peak experience of sexual pleasure, since the orgasm was made an object of intention, and an object of attention as well, instead of remaining an unintended effect of unreflected dedication and surrender to the partner. After undergoing short-term logotherapy, the patient's excessive attention and intention of her ability to experience orgasm had been "dereflected," to introduce another logotherapeutic term. When her attention was refocused toward the proper object, i.e., the partner, orgasm established itself spontaneously.[9]

---

9. In order to treat cases of sexual impotence, a specific logotherapeutic technique has been developed, based on the theory of hyper-intention and hyper-reflection as sketched above (Viktor E. Frankl, "The Pleasure Principle and Sexual Neurosis," *The International Journal of Sexology*, Vol. 5, No. 3 [1952], pp. 128–30). Of course, this cannot be dealt with in this brief presentation of the principles of logotherapy.

Logotherapy bases its technique called "paradoxical in-tention" on the twofold fact that fear brings about that which one is afraid of, and that hyper-intention makes impossible what one wishes. In German I described paradoxical inten-tion as early as 1939.[10] In this approach the phobic patient is invited to intend, even if only for a moment, precisely that which he fears.

Let me recall a case. A young physician consulted me be-cause of his fear of perspiring. Whenever he expected an out-break of perspiration, this anticipatory anxiety was enough to precipitate excessive sweating. In order to cut this circle formation I advised the patient, in the event that sweating should recur, to resolve deliberately to show people how much he could sweat. A week later he returned to report that whenever he met anyone who triggered his anticipatory anx-iety, he said to himself, "I only sweated out a quart before, but now I'm going to pour at least ten quarts!" The result was that, after suffering from his phobia for four years, he was able, af-ter a single session, to free himself permanently of it within one week.

The reader will note that this procedure consists of a reversal of the patient's attitude, inasmuch as his fear is re-placed by a paradoxical wish. By this treatment, the wind is taken out of the sails of the anxiety.

Such a procedure, however, must make use of the specifi-cally human capacity for self-detachment inherent in a sense

---

10. Viktor E. Frankl, "Zur medikamentösen Unterstützung der Psycho-therapie bei Neurosen," *Schweizer Archiv für Neurologie und Psychiatrie*, Vol. 43, pp. 26–31.

of humor. This basic capacity to detach one from oneself is actualized whenever the logotherapeutic technique called paradoxical intention is applied. At the same time, the patient is enabled to put himself at a distance from his own neurosis. A statement consistent with this is found in Gordon W. Allport's book, *The Individual and His Religion*: "The neurotic who learns to laugh at himself may be on the way to self-management, perhaps to cure."[11] Paradoxical intention is the empirical validation and clinical application of Allport's statement.

A few more case reports may serve to clarify this method further. The following patient was a bookkeeper who had been treated by many doctors and in several clinics without any therapeutic success. When he was admitted to my hospital department, he was in extreme despair, confessing that he was close to suicide. For some years, he had suffered from a writer's cramp which had recently become so severe that he was in danger of losing his job. Therefore, only immediate short-term therapy could alleviate the situation. In starting treatment, Dr. Eva Kozdera recommended to the patient that he do just the opposite of what he usually had done; namely, instead of trying to write as neatly and legibly as possible, to write with the worst possible scrawl. He was advised to say to himself, "Now I will show people what a good scribbler I am!" And at the moment in which he deliberately tried to scribble, he was unable to do so. "I tried to scrawl but simply could not do it," he said the next day. Within forty-eight hours the patient was in this way freed from his writer's cramp, and re-

---

11. New York, The Macmillan Co., 1956, p. 92.

mained free for the observation period after he had been treated. He is a happy man again and fully able to work.

A similar case, dealing, however, with speaking rather than writing, was related to me by a colleague in the Laryngological Department of the Vienna Poliklinik Hospital. It was the most severe case of stuttering he had come across in his many years of practice. Never in his life, as far as the stutterer could remember, had he been free from his speech trouble, even for a moment, except once. This happened when he was twelve years old and had hooked a ride on a streetcar. When caught by the conductor, he thought that the only way to escape would be to elicit his sympathy, and so he tried to demonstrate that he was just a poor stuttering boy. At that moment, when he tried to stutter, he was unable to do it. Without meaning to, he had practiced paradoxical intention, though not for therapeutic purposes.

However, this presentation should not leave the impression that paradoxical intention is effective only in monosymptomatic cases. By means of this logotherapeutic technique, my staff at the Vienna Poliklinik Hospital has succeeded in bringing relief even in obsessive-compulsive neuroses of a most severe degree and duration. I refer, for instance, to a woman sixty-five years of age who had suffered for sixty years from a washing compulsion. Dr. Eva Kozdera started logotherapeutic treatment by means of paradoxical intention, and two months later the patient was able to lead a normal life. Before admission to the Neurological Department of the Vienna Poliklinik Hospital, she had confessed, "Life was hell for me." Handicapped by her compulsion and bacteriophobic obsession, she finally remained in bed all day unable to do any housework. It would not be accurate to say that she is now completely free of symptoms, for an obsession may come to her mind. However, she is able to "joke about it," as she says; in short, to apply paradoxical intention.

Paradoxical intention can also be applied in cases of sleep disturbance. The fear of sleeplessness[12] results in a hyper-intention to fall asleep, which, in turn, incapacitates the patient to do so. To overcome this particular fear, I usually advise the patient not to try to sleep but rather to try to do just the opposite, that is, to stay awake as long as possible. In other words, the hyper-intention to fall asleep, arising from the anticipatory anxiety of not being able to do so, must be replaced by the paradoxical intention not to fall asleep, which soon will be followed by sleep.

Paradoxical intention is no panacea. Yet it lends itself as a useful tool in treating obsessive-compulsive and phobic conditions, especially in cases with underlying anticipatory anxiety. Moreover, it is a short-term therapeutic device. However, one should not conclude that such a short-term therapy necessarily results in only temporary therapeutic effects. One of "the more common illusions of Freudian orthodoxy," to quote the late Emil A. Gutheil, "is that the durability of results corresponds to the length of therapy."[13] In my files there is, for instance, the case report of a patient to whom paradoxical intention was administered more than twenty years ago;

---

12. The fear of sleeplessness is, in the majority of cases, due to the patient's ignorance of the fact that the organism provides itself *by itself* with the minimum amount of sleep really needed.

13. *American Journal of Psychotherapy*, 10 (1956), p. 134.

the therapeutic effect proved to be, nevertheless, a permanent one.

One of the most remarkable facts is that paradoxical intention is effective regardless of the etiological basis of the case concerned. This confirms a statement once made by Edith Weisskopf-Joelson: "Although traditional psychotherapy has insisted that therapeutic practices have to be based on findings on etiology, it is possible that certain factors might cause neuroses during early childhood and that entirely different factors might relieve neuroses during adulthood."[14]

As for the actual causation of neuroses, apart from constitutional elements, whether somatic or psychic in nature, such feedback mechanisms as anticipatory anxiety seem to be a major pathogenic factor. A given symptom is responded to by a phobia, the phobia triggers the symptom, and the symptom, in turn, reinforces the phobia. A similar chain of events, however, can be observed in obsessive-compulsive cases in which the patient fights the ideas which haunt him.[15] Thereby, however, he increases their power to disturb him, since pressure precipitates counterpressure. Again the symptom is reinforced! On the other hand, as soon as the patient stops fighting his obsessions and instead tries to ridicule them by dealing with them in an ironical way—by applying paradoxical intention—*the vicious circle is cut*, the symptom

---

14. "Some Comments on a Viennese School of Psychiatry," *The Journal of Abnormal and Social Psychology*, 51 (1955), pp. 701–3.

15. This is often motivated by the patient's fear that his obsessions indicate an imminent or even actual psychosis; the patient is not aware of the empirical fact that an obsessive-compulsive neurosis is immunizing him against a formal psychosis rather than endangering him in this direction.

diminishes and finally atrophies. In the fortunate case where there is no existential vacuum which invites and elicits the symptom, the patient will not only succeed in ridiculing his neurotic fear but finally will succeed in completely ignoring it.

As we see, anticipatory anxiety has to be counteracted by paradoxical intention; hyper-intention as well as hyper-reflection have to be counteracted by dereflection; dereflection, however, ultimately is not possible except by the patient's orientation toward his specific vocation and mission in life.[16]

It is not the neurotic's self-concern, whether pity or contempt, which breaks the circle formation; the cue to cure is self-transcendence!

### The Collective Neurosis

Every age has its own collective neurosis, and every age needs its own psychotherapy to cope with it. The existential vacuum which is the mass neurosis of the present time can be described as a private and personal form of nihilism; for nihilism can be defined as the contention that being has no meaning. As for psychotherapy, however, it will never be able to cope with this state of affairs on a mass scale if it does not keep itself free from the impact and influence of the contemporary trends of a nihilistic philosophy; otherwise it represents a symptom of the mass neurosis rather than its possible

---

16. This conviction is supported by Allport who once said, "As the focus of striving shifts from the conflict to selfless goals, the life as a whole becomes sounder even though the neurosis may never completely disappear" (op. cit., p. 95).

cure. Psychotherapy would not only reflect a nihilistic philosophy but also, even though unwillingly and unwittingly,
transmit to the patient what is actually a caricature rather
than a true picture of man.

First of all, there is a danger inherent in the teaching of
man's "nothingbutness," the theory that man is nothing but
the result of biological, psychological and sociological conditions, or the product of heredity and environment. Such a
view of man makes a neurotic believe what he is prone to believe anyway, namely, that he is the pawn and victim of outer
influences or inner circumstances. This neurotic fatalism is
fostered and strengthened by a psychotherapy which denies
that man is free.

To be sure, a human being is a finite thing, and his freedom is restricted. It is not freedom from conditions, but it *is*
freedom to take a stand toward the conditions. As I once put
it: "As a professor in two fields, neurology and psychiatry, I am
fully aware of the extent to which man is subject to biological,
psychological and sociological conditions. But in addition to
being a professor in two fields I am a survivor of four camps
—concentration camps, that is—and as such I also bear witness to the unexpected extent to which man is capable of de-
fying and braving even the worst conditions conceivable."[17]

### Critique of Pan-Determinism

Psychoanalysis has often been blamed for its so-called pan-
sexualism. I, for one, doubt whether this reproach has ever

---

17. "Value Dimensions in Teaching," a color television film produced by
Hollywood Animators, Inc., for the California Junior College Association.

been legitimate. However, there is something which seems to me to be an even more erroneous and dangerous assumption, namely, that which I call "pan-determinism." By that I mean the view of man which disregards his capacity to take a stand toward any conditions whatsoever. Man is *not* fully conditioned and determined but rather determines himself whether he gives in to conditions or stands up to them. In other words, man is ultimately self-determining. Man does not simply exist but always decides what his existence will be, what he will become in the next moment.

By the same token, every human being has the freedom to change at any instant. Therefore, we can predict his future only within the large framework of a statistical survey referring to a whole group; the individual personality, however, remains essentially unpredictable. The basis for any predictions would be represented by biological, psychological or sociological conditions. Yet one of the main features of human existence is the capacity to rise above such conditions, to grow beyond them. Man is capable of changing the world for the better if possible, and of changing himself for the better if necessary.

Let me cite the case of Dr. J. He was the only man I ever encountered in my whole life whom I would dare to call a Mephistophelean being, a satanic figure. At that time he was generally called "the mass murderer of Steinhof" (the large mental hospital in Vienna). When the Nazis started their euthanasia program, he held all the strings in his hands and was so fanatic in the job assigned to him that he tried not to let one single psychotic individual escape the gas chamber. After the war, when I came back to Vienna, I asked what had happened to Dr. J. "He had been imprisoned by the Russians in one of the isolation cells of Steinhof," they told me. "The next day, however, the door of his cell stood open and Dr. J. was never seen again." Later I was convinced that, like others, he had with the help of his comrades made his way to South America. More recently, however, I was consulted by a former Austrian diplomat who had been imprisoned behind the Iron Curtain for many years, first in Siberia and then in the famous Lubianka prison in Moscow. While I was examining him neurologically, he suddenly asked me whether I happened to know Dr. J. After my affirmative reply he continued: "I made his acquaintance in Lubianka. There he died, at about the age of forty, from cancer of the urinary bladder. Before he died, however, he showed himself to be the best comrade you can imagine! He gave consolation to everybody. He lived up to the highest conceivable moral standard. He was the best friend I ever met during my long years in prison!"

This is the story of Dr. J., "the mass murderer of Steinhof." How can we dare to predict the behavior of man? We may predict the movements of a machine, of an automaton; more than this, we may even try to predict the mechanisms or "dynamisms" of the human *psyche* as well. But man is more than *psyche*.

Freedom, however, is not the last word. Freedom is only part of the story and half of the truth. Freedom is but the negative aspect of the whole phenomenon whose positive aspect is responsibleness. In fact, freedom is in danger of degenerating into mere arbitrariness unless it is lived in terms of responsibleness. That is why *I recommend that the Statue of Liberty on the East Coast be supplemented by a Statue of Responsibility on the West Coast.*

## The Psychiatric Credo

There is nothing conceivable which would so condition a man as to leave him without the slightest freedom. Therefore, a residue of freedom, however limited it may be, is left to man in neurotic and even psychotic cases. Indeed, the innermost core of the patient's personality is not even touched by a psychosis.

An incurably psychotic individual may lose his usefulness but yet retain the dignity of a human being. This is my psychiatric credo. Without it I should not think it worthwhile to be a psychiatrist. For whose sake? Just for the sake of a damaged brain machine which cannot be repaired? If the patient were not definitely more, euthanasia would be justified.

## Psychiatry Rehumanized

For too long a time—for half a century, in fact—psychiatry tried to interpret the human mind merely as a mechanism, and consequently the therapy of mental disease merely in terms of a technique. I believe this dream has been dreamt out. What now begins to loom on the horizon are not the sketches of a psychologized medicine but rather those of a humanized psychiatry.

A doctor, however, who would still interpret his own role mainly as that of a technician would confess that he sees in his patient nothing more than a machine, instead of seeing the human being behind the disease!

A human being is not one thing among others; *things* determine each other, but *man* is ultimately self-determining.

What he becomes—within the limits of endowment and environment—he has made out of himself. In the concentration camps, for example, in this living laboratory and on this testing ground, we watched and witnessed some of our comrades behave like swine while others behaved like saints. Man has both potentialities within himself; which one is actualized depends on decisions but not on conditions.

Our generation is realistic, for we have come to know man as he really is. After all, man is that being who invented the gas chambers of Auschwitz; however, he is also that being who entered those gas chambers upright, with the Lord's Prayer or the *Shema Yisrael* on his lips.

# POSTSCRIPT
# 1984

*Dedicated to the memory of
Edith Weisskopf-Joelson, whose
pioneering efforts in logotherapy
in the United States began as early
as 1955 and whose contributions
to the field have been invaluable.*

# THE CASE FOR A
# TRAGIC OPTIMISM

LET US FIRST ASK OURSELVES WHAT SHOULD BE understood
by "a tragic optimism." In brief it means that one is, and remains, optimistic in spite of the "tragic triad," as it is called in
logotherapy, a triad which consists of those aspects of human
existence which may be circumscribed by: (1) pain; (2) guilt;
and (3) death. This chapter, in fact, raises the question, How
is it possible to say yes to life in spite of all that? How, to pose
the question differently, can life retain its potential meaning
in spite of its tragic aspects? After all, "saying yes to life in spite
of everything," to use the phrase in which the title of a German book of mine is couched, presupposes that life is potentially meaningful under any conditions, even those which are
most miserable. And this in turn presupposes the human capacity to creatively turn life's negative aspects into something
positive or constructive. In other words, what matters is to
make the best of any given situation. "The best," however, is
that which in Latin is called *optimum*—hence the reason I
speak of a tragic optimism, that is, an optimism in the face
of tragedy and in view of the human potential which at its

---

This chapter is based on a lecture I presented at the Third World Congress of
Logotherapy, Regensburg University, West Germany, June 1983.

best always allows for: (1) turning suffering into a human achievement and accomplishment; (2) deriving from guilt the opportunity to change oneself for the better; and (3) deriving from life's transitoriness an incentive to take responsible action.

It must be kept in mind, however, that optimism is not anything to be commanded or ordered. One cannot even force oneself to be optimistic indiscriminately, against all odds, against all hope. And what is true for hope is also true for the other two components of the triad inasmuch as faith and love cannot be commanded or ordered either.

To the European, it is a characteristic of the American culture that, again and again, one is commanded and ordered to "be happy." But happiness cannot be pursued; it must ensue. One must have a reason to "be happy." Once the reason is found, however, one becomes happy automatically. As we see, a human being is not one in pursuit of happiness but rather in search of a reason to become happy, last but not least, through actualizing the potential meaning inherent and dormant in a given situation.

This need for a reason is similar in another specifically human phenomenon—laughter. If you want anyone to laugh you have to provide him with a reason, e.g., you have to tell him a joke. In no way is it possible to evoke real laughter by urging him, or having him urge himself, to laugh. Doing so would be the same as urging people posed in front of a camera to say "cheese," only to find that in the finished photographs their faces are frozen in artificial smiles.

In logotherapy, such a behavior pattern is called "hyperintention." It plays an important role in the causation of sexual neurosis, be it frigidity or impotence. The more a patient, instead of forgetting himself through giving himself, directly strives for orgasm, i.e., sexual pleasure, the more this pursuit of sexual pleasure becomes self-defeating. Indeed, what is called "the pleasure principle" is, rather, a fun-spoiler.

Once an individual's search for a meaning is successful, it not only renders him happy but also gives him the capability to cope with suffering. And what happens if one's groping for a meaning has been in vain? This may well result in a fatal condition. Let us recall, for instance, what sometimes happened in extreme situations such as prisoner-of-war camps or concentration camps. In the first, as I was told by American soldiers, a behavior pattern crystallized to which they referred as "give-up-itis." In the concentration camps, this behavior was paralleled by those who one morning, at five, refused to get up and go to work and instead stayed in the hut, on the straw wet with urine and feces. Nothing—neither warnings nor threats—could induce them to change their minds. And then something typical occurred: they took out a cigarette from deep down in a pocket where they had hidden it and started smoking. At that moment we knew that for the next forty-eight hours or so we would watch them dying. Meaning orientation had subsided, and consequently the seeking of immediate pleasure had taken over.

Is this not reminiscent of another parallel, a parallel that confronts us day by day? I think of those youngsters who, on a worldwide scale, refer to themselves as the "no future" generation. To be sure, it is not just a cigarette to which they resort; it is drugs.

In fact, the drug scene is one aspect of a more general

mass phenomenon, namely the feeling of meaninglessness resulting from a frustration of our existential needs which in turn has become a universal phenomenon in our industrial societies. Today it is not only logotherapists who claim that the feeling of meaninglessness plays an ever increasing role in the etiology of neurosis. As Irvin D. Yalom of Stanford University states in *Existential Psychotherapy*: "Of forty consecutive patients applying for therapy at a psychiatric outpatient clinic...twelve (30 percent) had some major problem involving meaning (as adjudged from self-ratings, therapists, or independent judges)."[1] Thousands of miles east of Palo Alto, the situation differs only by 1 percent; the most recent pertinent statistics indicate that in Vienna, 29 percent of the population complain that meaning is missing from their lives.

As to the causation of the feeling of meaninglessness, one may say, albeit in an oversimplifying vein, that people have enough to live by but nothing to live for; they have the means but no meaning. To be sure, some do not even have the means. In particular, I think of the mass of people who are today unemployed. Fifty years ago, I published a study[2] devoted to a specific type of depression I had diagnosed in cases of young patients suffering from what I called "unemployment neurosis." And I could show that this neurosis really originated in a twofold erroneous identification: being jobless was equated with being useless, and being useless was equated with having a meaningless life. Consequently, when-

---

1. Basic Books, New York, 1980, p. 448.
2. "Wirtschaftskrise und Seelenleben vom Standpunkt des Jugendberaters," *Sozialärztliche Rundschau*, Vol. 4 (1933), pp. 43–46.

ever I succeeded in persuading the patients to volunteer in youth organizations, adult education, public libraries and the like—in other words, as soon as they could fill their abundant free time with some sort of unpaid but meaningful activity—their depression disappeared although their economic situation had not changed and their hunger was the same. The truth is that man does not live by welfare alone.

Along with unemployment neurosis, which is triggered by an individual's socioeconomic situation, there are other types of depression which are traceable back to psychodynamic or biochemical conditions, whichever the case may be. Accordingly, psychotherapy and pharmacotherapy are indicated respectively. Insofar as the feeling of meaninglessness is concerned, however, we should not overlook and forget that, per se, it is not a matter of pathology; rather than being the sign and symptom of a neurosis, it is, I would say, the proof of one's humanness. But although it is not caused by anything pathological, it may well cause a pathological reaction; in other words, it is potentially pathogenic. Just consider the mass neurotic syndrome so pervasive in the young generation: there is ample empirical evidence that the three facets of this syndrome—depression, aggression, addiction —are due to what is called in logotherapy "the existential vacuum," a feeling of emptiness and meaninglessness.

It goes without saying that not each and every case of depression is to be traced back to a feeling of meaninglessness, nor does suicide—in which depression sometimes eventuates—always result from an existential vacuum. But even if each and every case of suicide had not been *undertaken* out of a feeling of meaninglessness, it may well be that an individual's impulse to take his life would have been *overcome* had he been aware of some meaning and purpose worth living for.

If, thus, a strong meaning orientation plays a decisive role in the prevention of suicide, what about intervention in cases in which there is a suicide risk? As a young doctor I spent four years in Austria's largest state hospital where I was in charge of the pavilion in which severely depressed patients were accommodated—most of them having been admitted after a suicide attempt. I once calculated that I must have explored twelve thousand patients during those four years. What accumulated was quite a store of experience from which I still draw whenever I am confronted with someone who is prone to suicide. I explain to such a person that patients have repeatedly told me how happy they were that the suicide attempt had not been successful; weeks, months, years later, they told me, it turned out that there *was* a solution to their problem, an answer to their question, a meaning to their life. "Even if things only take such a good turn in one of a thousand cases," my explanation continues, "who can guarantee that in your case it will not happen one day, sooner or later? But in the first place, you have to live to see the day on which it may happen, so you have to survive in order to see that day dawn, and from now on the responsibility for survival does not leave you."

Regarding the second facet of the mass neurotic syndrome —aggression—let me cite an experiment once conducted by Carolyn Wood Sherif. She had succeeded in artificially building up mutual aggressions between groups of boy scouts, and observed that the aggressions only subsided when the youngsters dedicated themselves to a collective purpose—that is, the joint task of dragging out of the mud a carriage in which food had to be brought to their camp. Immediately, they were not only challenged but also united by a meaning they had to fulfill.[3]

As for the third issue, addiction, I am reminded of the findings presented by Annemarie von Forstmeyer who noted that, as evidenced by tests and statistics, 90 percent of the alcoholics she studied had suffered from an abysmal feeling of meaninglessness. Of the drug addicts studied by Stanley Krippner, 100 percent believed that "things seemed meaningless."[4]

Now let us turn to the question of meaning itself. To begin with, I would like to clarify that, in the first place, the logotherapist is concerned with the potential meaning inherent and dormant in all the single situations one has to face throughout his or her life. Therefore, I will not be elaborating here on the meaning of one's life as a whole, although I do not deny that such a long-range meaning does exist. To invoke an analogy, consider a movie: it consists of thousands upon thousands of individual pictures, and each of them makes sense and carries a meaning, yet the meaning of the whole film cannot be seen before its last sequence is shown. However, we cannot understand the whole film without having

---

3. For further information on this experiment, see Viktor E. Frankl, *The Unconscious God*, New York, Simon and Schuster, 1978, p. 140; and Viktor E. Frankl, *The Unheard Cry for Meaning*, New York, Simon and Schuster, 1978, p. 36.

4. For further information, see *The Unconscious God*, pp. 97–100; and *The Unheard Cry for Meaning*, pp. 26–28.

first understood each of its components, each of the individual pictures. Isn't it the same with life? Doesn't the final meaning of life, too, reveal itself, if at all, only at its end, on the verge of death? And doesn't this final meaning, too, depend on whether or not the potential meaning of each single situation has been actualized to the best of the respective individual's knowledge and belief?

The fact remains that meaning, and its perception, as seen from the logotherapeutic angle, is completely down to earth rather than afloat in the air or resident in an ivory tower. Sweepingly, I would locate the cognition of meaning—of the personal meaning of a concrete situation—midway between an "aha" experience along the lines of Karl Bühler's concept and a Gestalt perception, say, along the lines of Max Wertheimer's theory. The perception of meaning differs from the classical concept of Gestalt perception insofar as the latter implies the sudden awareness of a "figure" on a "ground," whereas the perception of meaning, as I see it, more specifically boils down to becoming aware of a possibility against the background of reality or, to express it in plain words, to becoming aware of *what can be done* about a given situation.

And how does a human being go about *finding* meaning? As Charlotte Bühler has stated: "All we can do is study the lives of people who seem to have found their answers to the questions of what ultimately human life is about as against those who have not."[5] In addition to such a biographical approach, however, we may as well embark on a biological approach.

5. "Basic Theoretical Concepts of Humanistic Psychology," *American Psychologist*, XXVI (April 1971), p. 378.

Logotherapy conceives of conscience as a prompter which, if need be, indicates the direction in which we have to move in a given life situation. In order to carry out such a task, conscience must apply a measuring stick to the situation one is confronted with, and this situation has to be evaluated in the light of a set of criteria, in the light of a hierarchy of values. These values, however, cannot be espoused and adopted by us on a conscious level—they are something that we *are*. They have crystallized in the course of the evolution of our species; they are founded on our biological past and are rooted in our biological depth. Konrad Lorenz might have had something similar in mind when he developed the concept of a biological *a priori*, and when both of us recently discussed my own view on the biological foundation of the valuing process, he enthusiastically expressed his accord. In any case, if a pre-reflective axiological self-understanding exists, we may assume that it is ultimately anchored in our biological heritage.

As logotherapy teaches, there are three main avenues on which one arrives at meaning in life. The first is by creating a work or by doing a deed. The second is by experiencing something or encountering someone; in other words, meaning can be found not only in work but also in love. Edith Weisskopf-Joelson observed in this context that the logotherapeutic "notion that experiencing can be as valuable as achieving is therapeutic because it compensates for our one-sided emphasis on the external world of achievement at the expense of the internal world of experience."[6]

---

6. "The Place of Logotherapy in the World Today," *The International Forum for Logotherapy*, Vol. 1, No. 3 (1980), pp. 3–7.

Most important, however, is the third avenue to meaning in life: even the helpless victim of a hopeless situation, facing a fate he cannot change, may rise above himself, may grow beyond himself, and by so doing change himself. He may turn a personal tragedy into a triumph. Again it was Edith Weisskopf-Joelson who, as mentioned on p. 114, once expressed the hope that logotherapy "may help counteract certain unhealthy trends in the present-day culture of the United States, where the incurable sufferer is given very little opportunity to be proud of his suffering and to consider it ennobling rather than degrading" so that "he is not only unhappy, but also ashamed of being unhappy."

For a quarter of a century I ran the neurological department of a general hospital and bore witness to my patients' capacity to turn their predicaments into human achievements. In addition to such practical experience, empirical evidence is also available which supports the possibility that one may find meaning in suffering. Researchers at the Yale University School of Medicine "have been impressed by the number of prisoners of war of the Vietnam war who explicitly claimed that although their captivity was extraordinarily stressful—filled with torture, disease, malnutrition, and solitary confinement—they nevertheless...benefited from the captivity experience, seeing it as a growth experience."[7]

But the most powerful arguments in favor of "a tragic optimism" are those which in Latin are called *argumenta ad*

---

7. W. H. Sledge, J. A. Boydstun and A. J. Rabe, "Self-Concept Changes Related to War Captivity," *Arch. Gen. Psychiatry*, 37 (1980), pp. 430–443.

*hominem.* Jerry Long, to cite an example, is a living testimony to "the defiant power of the human spirit," as it is called in logotherapy.[8] To quote the *Texarkana Gazette*, "Jerry Long has been paralyzed from his neck down since a diving accident which rendered him a quadriplegic three years ago. He was seventeen when the accident occurred. Today Long can use his mouth stick to type. He 'attends' two courses at Community College via a special telephone. The intercom allows Long to both hear and participate in class discussions. He also occupies his time by reading, watching television and writing." And in a letter I received from him, he writes: "I view my life as being abundant with meaning and purpose. The attitude that I adopted on that fateful day has become my personal credo for life: I broke my neck, it didn't break me. I am currently enrolled in my first psychology course in college. I believe that my handicap will only enhance my ability to help others. I know that without the suffering, the growth that I have achieved would have been impossible."

Is this to say that suffering is indispensable to the discovery of meaning? In no way. I only insist that meaning is available in spite of—nay, even through—suffering, provided, as noted in Part Two of this book, that the suffering is unavoidable. If it is avoidable, the meaningful thing to do is to remove its cause, for unnecessary suffering is masochistic rather than heroic. If, on the other hand, one cannot change a situation that causes his suffering, he can still choose his at-

---

8. "The Defiant Power of the Human Spirit" was in fact the title of a paper presented by Long at the Third World Congress of Logotherapy in June 1983.

titude.[9] Long had not chosen to break his neck, but he did decide not to let himself be broken by what had happened to him.

As we see, the priority stays with creatively changing the situation that causes us to suffer. But the superiority goes to the "know-how to suffer," if need be. And there is empirical evidence that—literally—the "man in the street" is of the same opinion. Austrian public-opinion pollsters recently reported that those held in highest esteem by most of the people interviewed are neither the great artists nor the great scientists, neither the great statesmen nor the great sports figures, but those who master a hard lot with their heads held high.

In turning to the second aspect of the tragic triad, namely guilt, I would like to depart from a theological concept that has always been fascinating to me. I refer to what is called *mysterium iniquitatis*, meaning, as I see it, that a crime in the final analysis remains inexplicable inasmuch as it cannot be fully traced back to biological, psychological and/or sociological factors. Totally explaining one's crime would be tantamount to explaining away his or her guilt and to seeing in him or her not a free and responsible human being but a machine

---

9. I won't forget an interview I once heard on Austrian TV, given by a Polish cardiologist who, during World War II, had helped organize the Warsaw ghetto upheaval. "What a heroic deed," exclaimed the reporter. "Listen," calmly replied the doctor, "to take a gun and shoot is no great thing; but if the SS leads you to a gas chamber or to a mass grave to execute you on the spot, and you can't do anything about it—except for going your way with dignity— you see, this is what I would call heroism." Attitudinal heroism, so to speak.

to be repaired. Even criminals themselves abhor this treatment and prefer to be held responsible for their deeds. From a convict serving his sentence in an Illinois penitentiary I received a letter in which he deplored that "the criminal never has a chance to explain himself. He is offered a variety of excuses to choose from. Society is blamed and in many instances the blame is put on the victim." Furthermore, when I addressed the prisoners in San Quentin, I told them that "you are human beings like me, and as such you were free to commit a crime, to become guilty. Now, however, you are responsible for overcoming guilt by rising above it, by growing beyond yourselves, by changing for the better." They felt understood.[10] And from Frank E.W., an ex-prisoner, I received a note which stated that he had "started a logotherapy group for ex-felons. We are 27 strong and the newer ones are staying out of prison through the peer strength of those of us from the original group. Only one returned—and he is now free."[11]

As for the concept of collective guilt, I personally think that it is totally unjustified to hold one person responsible for the behavior of another person or a collective of persons. Since the end of World War II I have not become weary of publicly arguing against the collective guilt concept.[12] Sometimes, however, it takes a lot of didactic tricks to detach people from their superstitions. An American woman once

---

10. See also Joseph B. Fabry, *The Pursuit of Meaning*, New York, Harper and Row, 1980.

11. Cf. Viktor E. Frankl, *The Unheard Cry for Meaning*, New York, Simon and Schuster, 1978, pp. 42–43.

12. See also Viktor E. Frankl, *Psychotherapy and Existentialism*, New York, Simon and Schuster, 1967.

confronted me with the reproach, "How can you still write some of your books in German, Adolf Hitler's language?" In response, I asked her if she had knives in her kitchen, and when she answered that she did, I acted dismayed and shocked, exclaiming, "How can you still use knives after so many killers have used them to stab and murder their victims?" She stopped objecting to my writing books in German.

The third aspect of the tragic triad concerns death. But it concerns life as well, for at any time each of the moments of which life consists is dying, and that moment will never recur. And yet is not this transitoriness a reminder that challenges us to make the best possible use of each moment of our lives? It certainly is, and hence my imperative: *Live as if you were living for the second time and had acted as wrongly the first time as you are about to act now.*

In fact, the opportunities to act properly, the potentialities to fulfill a meaning, are affected by the irreversibility of our lives. But also the potentialities alone are so affected. For as soon as we have used an opportunity and have actualized a potential meaning, we have done so once and for all. We have rescued it into the past wherein it has been safely delivered and deposited. In the past, nothing is irretrievably lost, but rather, on the contrary, everything is irrevocably stored and treasured. To be sure, people tend to see only the stubble fields of transitoriness but overlook and forget the full granaries of the past into which they have brought the harvest of their lives: the deeds done, the loves loved, and last but not least, the sufferings they have gone through with courage and dignity.

From this one may see that there is no reason to pity old people. Instead, young people should envy them. It is true that the old have no opportunities, no possibilities in the future. But they have more than that. Instead of possibilities in the future, they have realities in the past—the potentialities they have actualized, the meanings they have fulfilled, the values they have realized—and nothing and nobody can ever remove these assets from the past.

In view of the possibility of finding meaning in suffering, life's meaning is an unconditional one, at least potentially. That unconditional meaning, however, is paralleled by the unconditional value of each and every person. It is that which warrants the indelible quality of the dignity of man. Just as life remains potentially meaningful under any conditions, even those which are most miserable, so too does the value of each and every person stay with him or her, and it does so because it is based on the values that he or she has realized in the past, and is not contingent on the usefulness that he or she may or may not retain in the present.

More specifically, this usefulness is usually defined in terms of functioning for the benefit of society. But today's society is characterized by achievement orientation, and consequently it adores people who are successful and happy and, in particular, it adores the young. It virtually ignores the value of all those who are otherwise, and in so doing blurs the decisive difference between being valuable in the sense of dignity and being valuable in the sense of usefulness. If one is not cognizant of this difference and holds that an individual's value stems only from his present usefulness, then, believe me, one owes it only to personal inconsistency not to plead for euthanasia along the lines of Hitler's program, that is to say, "mercy" killing of all those who have lost their social usefulness, be it because of old age, incurable illness, mental deterioration, or whatever handicap they may suffer.

Confounding the dignity of man with mere usefulness arises from a conceptual confusion that in turn may be traced back to the contemporary nihilism transmitted on many an academic campus and many an analytical couch. Even in the setting of training analyses such an indoctrination may take place. Nihilism does not contend that there is nothing, but it states that everything is meaningless. And George A. Sargent was right when he promulgated the concept of "learned meaninglessness." He himself remembered a therapist who said, "George, you must realize that the world is a joke. There is no justice, everything is random. Only when you realize this will you understand how silly it is to take yourself seriously. There is no grand purpose in the universe. It just *is*. There's no particular meaning in what decision you make today about how to act."[13]

One must not generalize such a criticism. In principle, training is indispensable, but if so, therapists should see their task in immunizing the trainee against nihilism rather than inoculating him with the cynicism that is a defense mechanism against their own nihilism.

Logotherapists may even conform to some of the training and licensing requirements stipulated by the other schools of psychotherapy. In other words, one may howl with the

---

13. "Transference and Countertransference in Logotherapy," *The International Forum for Logotherapy*, Vol. 5, No. 2 (Fall/Winter 1982), pp. 115–18.

wolves, if need be, but when doing so, one should be, I would urge, a sheep in wolf's clothing. There is no need to become untrue to the basic concept of man and the principles of the philosophy of life inherent in logotherapy. Such a loyalty is not hard to maintain in view of the fact that, as Elisabeth S. Lukas once pointed out, "throughout the history of psychotherapy, there has never been a school as undogmatic as logotherapy."[14] And at the First World Congress of Logotherapy (San Diego, California, November 6–8, 1980) I argued not only for the rehumanization of psychotherapy but also for what I called "the degurufication of logotherapy." My interest does not lie in raising parrots that just rehash "their master's voice," but rather in passing the torch to "independent and inventive, innovative and creative spirits."

Sigmund Freud once asserted, "Let one attempt to expose a number of the most diverse people uniformly to hunger. With the increase of the imperative urge of hunger all individual differences will blur, and in their stead will appear the uniform expression of the one unstilled urge." Thank heaven, Sigmund Freud was spared knowing the concentration camps from the inside. His subjects lay on a couch designed in the plush style of Victorian culture, not in the filth of Auschwitz. *There*, the "individual differences" did *not* "blur" but, on the contrary, people became more different; people

---

14. Logotherapy is not imposed on those who are interested in psychotherapy. It is not comparable to an Oriental bazaar but rather to a supermarket. In the former, the customer is talked into buying something. In the latter, he is shown, and offered, various things from which he may pick what he deems usable and valuable.

unmasked themselves, both the swine and the saints. And to-day you need no longer hesitate to use the word "saints": think of Father Maximilian Kolbe who was starved and finally murdered by an injection of carbolic acid at Auschwitz and who in 1983 was canonized.

You may be prone to blame me for invoking examples that are the exceptions to the rule. *"Sed omnia praeclara tam difficilia quam rara sunt"* (but everything great is just as difficult to realize as it is rare to find) reads the last sentence of the *Ethics* of Spinoza. You may of course ask whether we really need to refer to "saints." Wouldn't it suffice just to refer to *decent* people? It is true that they form a minority. More than that, they always will remain a minority. And yet I see therein the very challenge to join the minority. For the world is in a bad state, but everything will become still worse unless each of us does his best.

So, let us be alert—alert in a twofold sense:

Since Auschwitz we know what man is capable of.

And since Hiroshima we know what is at stake.

# AFTERWORD

ON JANUARY 27, 2006, the sixty-first anniversary of the liberation of the Auschwitz death camp, where 1.5 million people died, nations around the world observed the first International Holocaust Remembrance Day. A few months later, they might well have celebrated the anniversary of one of the most abiding pieces of writing from that horrendous time. First published in German in 1946 as *A Psychologist Experiences the Concentration Camp* and later called *Say Yes to Life in Spite of Everything*, subsequent editions were supplemented by an introduction to logotherapy and a postscript on tragic optimism, or how to remain optimistic in the face of pain, guilt, and death. The English translation, first published in 1959, was called *Man's Search for Meaning*.

Viktor Frankl's book has now sold more than 12 million copies in a total of twenty-four languages. A 1991 Library of Congress/Book-of-the-Month-Club survey asking readers to name a "book that made a difference in your life" found *Man's Search for Meaning* among the ten most influential books in America. It has inspired religious and philosophical thinkers, mental-health professionals, teachers, students, and general readers from all walks of life. It is routinely assigned to college, graduate, and high school students in psychology, philosophy, history, literature, Holocaust studies, religion, and theology. What accounts for its pervasive influence and enduring value?

Viktor Frankl's life spanned nearly all of the twentieth century, from his birth in 1905 to his death in 1997. At the age of three he decided to become a physician. In his autobiographical reflections, he recalls that as a youth he would "think for some minutes about the meaning of life. Particularly about the meaning of the coming day and its meaning for *me*."

As a teenager Frankl was fascinated by philosophy, experimental psychology, and psychoanalysis. To supplement his high school classes, he attended adult-education classes and began a correspondence with Sigmund Freud that led Freud to submit a manuscript of Frankl's to the *International Journal of Psychoanalysis*. The article was accepted and later published. That same year, at age sixteen, Frankl attended an adult-education workshop on philosophy. The instructor, recognizing Frankl's precocious intellect, invited him to give a lecture on the meaning of life. Frankl told the audience that "It is we ourselves who must answer the questions that life asks of us, and to these questions we can respond only by being responsible for our existence." This belief became the cornerstone of Frankl's personal life and professional identity.

Under the influence of Freud's ideas, Frankl decided while he was still in high school to become a psychiatrist. Inspired in part by a fellow student who told him he had a gift for helping others, Frankl had begun to realize that he had a talent not only for diagnosing psychological problems, but also for discovering what motivates people.

Frankl's first counseling job was entirely his own—he founded Vienna's first private youth counseling program and worked with troubled youths. From 1930 to 1937 he worked as a psychiatrist at the University Clinic in Vienna, caring for suicidal patients. He sought to help his patients find a way to make their lives meaningful even in the face of depression or mental illness. By 1939 he was head of the department of neurology at Rothschild Hospital, the only Jewish hospital in Vienna.

In the early years of the war, Frankl's work at Rothschild gave him and his family some degree of protection from the threat of deportation. When the hospital was closed down by the National Socialist government, however, Frankl realized that they were at grave risk of being sent to a concentration camp. In 1942 the American consulate in Vienna informed him that he was eligible for a U.S. immigration visa. Although an escape from Austria would have enabled him to complete his book on logotherapy, he decided to let his visa lapse: he felt he should stay in Vienna for the sake of his aging parents. In September 1942, Frankl and his family were arrested and deported. Frankl spent the next three years at four different concentration camps—Theresienstadt, Auschwitz-Birkenau, Kaufering, and Türkheim, part of the Dachau complex.

It is important to note that Frankl's imprisonment was not the only impetus for *Man's Search for Meaning*. Before his deportation, he had already begun to formulate an argument that the quest for meaning is the key to mental health and human flourishing. As a prisoner, he was suddenly forced to assess whether his own life still had any meaning. His survival was a combined result of his will to live, his instinct for self-preservation, some generous acts of human decency, and shrewdness; of course, it also depended on blind luck, such as where he happened to be imprisoned, the whims of the guards, and arbitrary decisions about where to line up and who to trust or believe. However, something more was needed to overcome the deprivations and degradations of the camps. Frankl drew constantly upon uniquely human capacities such as inborn optimism, humor, psychological detachment, brief moments of solitude, inner freedom, and a steely resolve not to give up or commit suicide. He realized that he must try to live for the future, and he drew strength from loving thoughts of his wife and his deep desire to finish his book on logotherapy. He also found meaning in glimpses of beauty in nature and art. Most important, he realized that, no matter what happened, he retained the freedom to choose how to respond to his suffering. He saw this not merely as an option but as his and every person's responsibility to choose "the way in which he bears his burden."

Sometimes Frankl's ideas are inspirational, as when he explains how dying patients and quadriplegics come to terms with their fate. Others are aspirational, as when he asserts that a person finds meaning by "striving and struggling for a worthwhile goal, a freely chosen task." He shows how existential frustration provoked and motivated an unhappy diplomat to seek a new, more satisfying career. Frankl also uses moral exhortation, however, to call attention to "the gap between what one is and what one should become" and the idea that "man is responsible and must actualize the potential meaning of his life." He sees freedom and responsibility as two sides of the same coin. When he spoke to American audiences, Frankl was fond of saying, "I recommend that the Statue of Liberty on the East Coast be supplemented by a Statue of Responsibility on the West Coast." To achieve personal meaning, he says, one must transcend subjective pleasures by doing something that "points, and is directed, to something, or someone, other than oneself . . . by giving himself to a cause to serve or another person to love." Frankl himself chose to focus on his parents by staying in Vienna when he could have had safe passage to America. While he was in the same concentration camp as his father, Frankl managed to obtain morphine to ease his father's pain and stayed by his side during his dying days.

Even when confronted by loss and sadness, Frankl's optimism, his constant affirmation of and exuberance about life, led him to insist that hope and positive energy can turn challenges into triumphs. In *Man's Search for Meaning*, he hastens to add that suffering is not *necessary* to find meaning, only that "meaning is possible in spite of suffering." Indeed, he goes on to say that "to suffer unnecessarily is masochistic rather than heroic."

I first read *Man's Search for Meaning* as a philosophy professor in the mid-1960s. The book was brought to my attention by a Norwegian philosopher who had himself been incarcerated in a Nazi concentration camp. My colleague remarked how strongly he agreed with Frankl about the importance of nourishing one's inner freedom, embracing the value of beauty in nature, art, poetry, and literature, and feeling love for family and friends. But other personal choices, activities, relationships, hobbies, and even simple pleasures can also give meaning to life. Why, then, do some people find themselves feeling so empty? Frankl's wisdom here is worth emphasizing: it is a question of the *attitude* one takes toward life's challenges and opportunities, both large and small. A positive attitude enables a person to endure suffering and disappointment as well as enhance enjoyment and satisfaction. A negative attitude intensifies pain and deepens disappointments; it undermines and diminishes pleasure, happiness, and satisfaction; it may even lead to depression or physical illness.

My friend and former colleague Norman Cousins was a tireless advocate for the value of positive emotions in promoting health, and he warned of the danger that negative emotions may jeopardize it. Although some critics attacked Cousins's views as simplistic, subsequent research in psychoneuroimmunology has supported the ways in which positive emotions, expectations, and attitudes enhance our immune system. This research also reinforces Frankl's belief that one's approach to everything from life-threatening challenges to everyday situations helps to shape the meaning of our lives. The simple truth that Frankl so ardently promoted has profound significance for anyone who listens.

The choices humans make should be active rather than passive. In making personal choices we affirm our autonomy. "A human being is not one thing among others; *things* determine each other," Frankl writes, "but *man* is ultimately self determining. What he becomes—within the limits of endowment and environment—he has made out of himself." For example, the darkness of despair threatened to overwhelm a young Israeli soldier who had lost both his legs in the Yom Kippur War. He was drowning in depression and contemplating suicide. One day a friend noticed that his outlook had changed to hopeful serenity. The soldier attributed his transformation to reading *Man's Search for Meaning*. When he was told about the soldier, Frankl wondered whether "there may be such a thing as autobibliotherapy—healing through reading."

Frankl's comment hints at the reasons why *Man's Search for Meaning* has such a powerful impact on many readers. Persons facing existential challenges or crises may seek advice or guidance from family, friends, therapists, or religious counselors. Sometimes such advice is helpful; sometimes it is not. Persons facing difficult choices may not fully appreciate how much their own attitude interferes with the decision they need to make or the action they need to take. Frankl offers readers who are searching for answers to life's dilemmas a critical mandate: he does not tell people *what* to do, but why *they* must do it.

After his liberation in 1945 from the Türkheim camp, where he had nearly died of typhus, Frankl discovered that he was utterly alone. On the first day of his return to Vienna in August 1945, Frankl learned that his pregnant wife, Tilly, had died of sickness or starvation in the Bergen-Belsen concentration camp. Sadly, his parents and brother had all died in the camps. Overcoming his losses and inevitable depression, he remained in Vienna to resume his career as a psychiatrist—an unusual choice when so many others, especially Jewish psychoanalysts and psychiatrists, had emigrated to other countries. Several factors may have contributed to this decision: Frankl felt an intense connection to Vienna, especially to psychiatric patients who needed his help in the postwar period. He also believed strongly in reconciliation rather than revenge; he once remarked, "I do not forget any good deed done to me, and I do not carry a grudge for a bad one." Notably, he renounced the idea of collective guilt. Frankl was able to accept that his Viennese colleagues and neighbors may have known about or even participated in his persecution, and he did not condemn them for failing to join the resistance or die heroic deaths. Instead, he was deeply committed to the idea that even a vile Nazi criminal or a seemingly hopeless madman has the potential to transcend evil or insanity by making responsible choices.

He threw himself passionately into his work. In 1946 he reconstructed and revised the book that was destroyed when he was first deported *(The Doctor and the Soul)*, and that same year—in only nine days—he wrote *Man's Search for Meaning*. He hoped to cure through his writings the personal alienation and cultural malaise that plagued many individuals who felt an "inner emptiness" or a "void within themselves." Perhaps this flurry of professional activity helped Frankl to restore meaning to his own life.

Two years later he married Eleanore Schwindt, who, like his first wife, was a nurse. Unlike Tilly, who was Jewish, Elly was Catholic. Although this may have been mere coincidence, it was characteristic of Viktor Frankl to accept individuals regardless of their religious beliefs or secular convictions. His deep commitment to the uniqueness and dignity of each individual was illustrated by his admiration for Freud and Adler even though he disagreed with their philosophical and psychological theories. He also valued his personal relationships with philosophers as radically different as Martin Heidegger, a reformed Nazi sympathizer, Karl Jaspers, an advocate of collective guilt, and Gabriel Marcel, a Catholic philosopher and writer. As a psychiatrist, Frankl avoided direct reference to his personal religious beliefs. He was fond of saying that the aim of psychiatry was the healing of the soul, leaving to religion the salvation of the soul.

He remained head of the neurology department at the Vienna Policlinic Hospital for twenty-five years and wrote more than thirty books for both professionals and general readers. He lectured widely in Europe, the Americas, Australia, Asia, and Africa; held professorships at Harvard, Stanford, and the University of Pittsburgh; and was Distinguished Professor of Logotherapy at the U.S. International University in San Diego. He met with politicians, world leaders such as Pope Paul VI, philosophers, students, teachers, and numerous individuals who had read and been inspired by his books. Even in his nineties, Frankl continued to engage in dialogue with visitors from all over the world and to respond personally to some of the hundreds of letters he received every week. Twenty-nine universities awarded him honorary degrees, and the American Psychiatric Association honored him with the Oskar Pfister Award.

Frankl is credited with establishing logotherapy as a psychiatric technique that uses existential analysis to help patients resolve their emotional conflicts. He stimulated many therapists to look beyond patients' past or present problems to help them choose productive futures by making personal choices and taking responsibility for them. Several generations of therapists were inspired by his humanistic insights, which gained influence as a result of Frankl's prolific writing, provocative lectures, and engaging personality. He encouraged others to use existential analysis creatively rather than to establish an official doctrine. He argued that therapists should focus on the specific needs of individual patients rather than extrapolate from abstract theories.

Despite a demanding schedule, Frankl also found time to take flying lessons and pursue his lifelong passion for mountain climbing. He joked that in contrast to Freud's and Adler's "depth psychology," which emphasizes delving into an individual's past and his or her unconscious instincts and desires, he practiced "height psychology," which focuses on a person's future and his or her conscious decisions and actions. His approach to psychotherapy stressed the importance of helping people to reach new heights of personal meaning through self-transcendence: the application of positive effort, technique, acceptance of limitations, and wise decisions. His goal was to provoke people into realizing that they could and should exercise their capacity for choice to achieve their own goals. Writing about tragic optimism, he cautioned us that "the world is in a bad state, but everything will become still worse unless each of us does his best."

Frankl was once asked to express in one sentence the meaning of his own life. He wrote the response on paper and asked his students to guess what he had written. After some moments of quiet reflection, a student surprised Frankl by saying, "The meaning of your life is to help others find the meaning of theirs."

"That was it, exactly," Frankl said. "Those are the very words I had written."

WILLIAM J. WINSLADE

*William J. Winslade is a philosopher, lawyer, and psychoanalyst who teaches psychiatry, medical ethics, and medical jurisprudence at the University of Texas Medical Branch in Galveston and the University of Houston Law Center.*